Foreword

The title of Dr Craggs's admirable work is properly challenging.

Thus I am returned to the origins of a dedication to a subject which – if not lifelong – has at least occupied considerably more than half a life. Already, in 1929, I was a good Handelian by way of choristerdom, and also something of a Brahmsian – inclined that way through the two-piano version of the St Anthony Variations. In a general sense – in the circles in which I moved – Brahms was then a 'modern' composer. In retrospect I understand that Elgar would have approved of Handel and Brahms as fundamental influences. C.S. Lang (a favourite pupil of Stanford) also came into my experience in that year, promoting Elgar with a compelling fervour. Lang was not only a teacher of unlimited enthusiasm, he was also an efficient (sometimes inspiring) composer, with the apparatus of composition always around him. We would perform his works, hot from the publisher, at school. Living near one composer was good preparation for gaining experience of others.

In what turned out to be a memorable summer, Lang took me to Stowe to meet P.A. Browne, then music master there. An Oxford Mus. D., Browne was a man of great musical perception and, as I soon was to learn, also a generous host. In that same summer I met him again on two occasions; once at dinner in the Richmond Club and later in Truro (also at his Club!), where I was visiting Guillaume Ormond, cathedral organist of happy memory. From those days a compelling memory is of Philip Browne playing long extracts from Elgar on the piano from full score. In later life he became the Chief Inspector for Schools at the then Ministry of Education. A fine and intellectual musician, his talent in that field was subsumed in his wider functions for the public good.

At the end of that summer I went, for the first time, to the Three Choirs Festival at Worcester. The City of Worcester then was small, unpretentious, modestly ancient (tourism had not yet been invented), traffic-empty, dusty and intimate. The cathedral ruled the place in every sense, so that music heard there assumed a character ordained by acoustics and consecrated by tradition. Elgar there was impelled towards his greatest choral works by a due sense of natural faith. In 1929, for the first time, I heard *Gerontius* and *The Kingdom* and (opening another channel for later exploration) Kodály's *Psalmus Hungaricus*.

The vocal score of *Gerontius* that I still use was bought in advance of the Gloucester Festival of 1931, but it was the Worcester Meeting of the following year that established a belief that Elgar – to be seen as well as heard – was a great composer. Not without influence in arriving at that point of no return was the privilege of brief acquaintance with some of his closest friends.

Posthumously a period of relative neglect, of consignment to the past, set in. Although Worcester – and its companion cities – in this sense remained *semper fidelis* a new generation of composers with new practices ruled.

A generation later, however, I received a letter which movingly demonstrates the turning wheel of fortune. From this letter, of 17 November 1962, I quote two relevant passages:

> ... I suppose I must be one of the few remaining musicians in Manchester who have played under Elgar. I did so on his last appearance here, in January (I think) 1933. The work was 'The dream of Gerontius' and I have never forgotten the impact of Elgar's personality, and the feeling one had of being in the presence of a *really* great musician and man. A truly memorable experience.

> ... I find interest growing again for Elgar, surprisingly enough in young people, and I wonder sometimes if those of us who have been loyal to him through an admittedly lean time are about to witness a grand revival of his music.

The rest is history – or some of it.

Percy M. Young

EDWARD ELGAR : A SOURCE BOOK

Elgar at Severn House, Hampstead, 1919

EDWARD ELGAR

A SOURCE BOOK

compiled by

STEWART R. CRAGGS

SCOLAR PRESS

Published by
SCOLAR PRESS
Gower House
Croft Road
Aldershot
Hants GU11 3HR
England

Ashgate Publishing Company
Old Post Road
Brookfield
Vermont 05036
USA

British Library Cataloguing-in-Publication data.

Edward Elgar: Source Book
  I. Craggs, Stewart R.
  016.78092

Library of Congress Cataloging-in-Publication Data

Craggs, Stewart R.
  Edward Elgar : a source book / compiled by Stewart R. Craggs.
    p.   cm.
  Discography: p.
  Includes bibliographical references (p.) and index.
  ISBN 0–85987–920–9
  1. Elgar, Edward, 1857–1934—Bibliography.   2. Elgar, Edward,
1857–1934—Discography.   I. Title.
ML134.E613C7   1995
016.780'92—dc20   94–22428
                  CIP
                  MN

ISBN 0 85967 920 9

Typeset in Goudy by Raven Typesetters, New Crane Street, Chester and printed in Great Britain by Biddles Ltd, Guildford.

To

PAUL S. WILSON

(1946–1992)

In memoriam

Previous Publications

William Walton: a thematic catalogue   OUP, 1977
William Alwyn: a catalogue   Bravura, 1985
Arthur Bliss: a bio-bibliography   Greenwood (USA), 1988
Richard Rodney Bennett: a bio-bibliography   Greenwood, 1989
William Walton: a catalogue   OUP, 1990
John McCabe: a bio-bibliography   Greenwood, 1991
William Walton: a source book   Scolar Press, 1993
John Ireland: a catalogue, discography and bibliography   OUP, 1993
Alun Hoddinott: a bio-bibliography   Greenwood, 1993

In preparation

William Mathias : a bio-bibliography   Greenwood
Arthur Bliss : a source book   Scolar Press
Malcolm Arnold : a bio-bibliography   Greenwood
Lennox Berkeley : a source book   Scolar Press
Peter Maxwell Davies : a source book   Scolar Press
John Ireland : a source book   Scolar Press
William Walton : a life in letters   Scolar Press
Benjamin Britten : a bio-bibliography   Greenwood

Contents

Compiler's Note

Having had a life-long admiration and love of Elgar's music, it was, I felt, an honour to be asked by Scolar Press, despite the very sad circumstances surrounding the commission, to take on the difficult task of finishing this volume.

Some years ago, I started to compile a catalogue and collect items for an Elgar bibliography, and the results of this research are included in the present volume. I felt then (and still do) that there was a need for a definitive catalogue of Elgar's music.

At the time of his death, Paul Wilson had collected many references for his bibliography, and these are accordingly included in the appropriate section. Unfortunately, Paul left no other indication about how the remainder of the volume was to be laid out, so the rest follows the practice of those already published in this important series.

My thanks go to the following for their help: Raymond Monk, one of the world's foremost authorities on the composer, for his help in so many ways and kind suggestions in the preparation of this volume, and Dr Percy Young, doyen of Elgar scholars, for generously agreeing to write the foreword; Richard Andrewes, Head of Music at Cambridge University Library; James Bennett, Curator, Elgar's Birthplace, Lower Broadheath; Christopher Bornet, Reference Librarian at the Royal College of Music; John Coggrave for bringing the existence of the novel about Elgar's Amazon journey to my attention; Dr John C. Dressler of the Music Department, Murray State University, Kentucky, USA; Dr Jeremy Dibble; Miss Jane Holmes; Mrs J. Kavanagh, Written Archives Officer at the BBC; Andrew Neil, Chairman of the Elgar Society; Michael Poppleston, Deputy City Librarian, Newcastle upon Tyne; and Eileen Burt, Humanities and Arts Librarian at Newcastle City Libraries, for allowing me access to their stacks.

Last, but not least, my thanks also go to Ellen Keeling, Senior Editor at

Scolar Press for her help, and my wife, Valerie, for her love, patience and support.

Stewart R. Craggs
Sunderland, May 1994

Alphabetical list of main compositions

Aspiration, *see* Scenes from the Bavarian Highlands (Op.27)
Aubade (Awake), *see* Nursery Suite (1930)
Ave Maria gratia plena (Op.2 no.2), 54
Ave Maria Stella (Op.2 no.3), 54
Ave Verum (Op.2 no.1), 20, 54

Bach Motif, 37
Ballet Music, 45
Banner of St. George, The (Op.33), 23, 24, 64, 107, 127, 132
Beau Brummel: incidental music, 34, 101, 108, 132
Bee, The, *see* Two Songs (Op.60)
Benedictus sit Deus Pater, 18, 49
Big Steamers, 95
Birthright, *see* Two Songs to words by John Drinkwater (1923)
Birthright, The (Stocks), 89
Bizarrerie (Op.13 no.2), 56
Black Knight, The (Op.25), 21, 22, 58, 127, 132
Blue Mountain, The: A Song of Australia, *see* Pageant of Empire (1924)
Brother, for thee He died, 45
Brook, The, 89
Busy-ness!, *see* Nursery Suite (1930)

Cadenza for C.H. Lloyd's Organ Concerto, 76
Café des ambassadeurs: La femme d'emballeur, *see* Five Quadrilles – Paris
    (1880)
Cantique (Op.3), 46
Caractacus (Op.35), 24, 36, 66, 133
Carillon (Op.75), 31, 89, 108, 126, 133
Carissima, 31, 88, 108, 134
Chanson de Matin (Op.15 no.2), 67, 109, 134
Chanson de Nuit (Op.15 no.1), 65, 109
Chantant, 37
Châtelet, *see* Five Quadrilles – Paris (1880)
Chariots of the Lord, The, 89
Child Asleep, A, 82
Christmas Greeting, A, (Op.52), 79, 125
Civic Fanfare, 34, 101, 109, 126, 134
Clapham Town End, 52

Twilight, *see* Song Cycle (Op.59)
Two Choral Songs (Op.71), 90
Two Choral Songs (Op.73), 91
Two movements for oboe and string quartet, 38
Two Part Songs (Op.26 nos.1 and 2), 62
Two Songs (Op.60), 84, 177
Two songs to words by John Drinkwater, 99

Une Idylle (Op.4 no.1), 52
Un Voix dans le Désert (Op.77), 31, 92, 177

Variations on an Original Theme ('Enigma') (Op.36), 24, 69, 121, 127, 177
Very easy melodious exercises in the first position (Op.22), 61
Vesper Voluntaries (Op.14), 21, 57
Vintage, *see* In a Vineyard (1909)
Virelai (Op.4 no.3), 52

Wagon Passes, The, *see* Nursery Suite (1930)
Waking, The, *see* Song Cycle (Op.59)
Wand of Youth Suite, The, No.1 (Op.1a), 28, 80, 122, 181
Wand of Youth Suite, The, No.2 (Op.1b), 29, 82, 122, 181
Wanderer, The, 99
Was it some Golden Star?, *see* Song Cycle (Op.59)
Wave, The, 62
Weary Wind of the West, 75
'Welsh' Overture, 73
When Swallows Fly, 105
Where Corals Lie, *see* Sea Pictures (Op.37)
Whether I find thee, *see* From the Greek Anthology (Op.45)
Wild Boars, The, *see* Wand of Youth Suite No.2 (Op.1b)
Wind at Dawn, The, 20, 56
Windlass Song, The, 91
Winter, *see* The Mill Wheel Songs
With Proud Thanksgiving, 93, 127, 181
Woodland Stream, The, 105

Yea, cast from me the heights of the mountain, *see* From the Greek Anthology (Op.45)

Zut! Zut! Zut!, 99, 181

Chronology

1821

September — William Henry Elgar (father) born in Dover

1848

January — W.H. Elgar marries Ann Greening (b.1822)

15 October — Henry John Elgar (Harry) born

1852

29 May — Lucy Ann Elgar born

1854

28 December — Susannah Mary (Pollie) Elgar born

1857

2 June — Edward William Elgar born at Broadheath

11 June — Baptised at St. George's R.C. Church, Worcester

1859

28 August — Frederick Joseph (Jo) Elgar born at Worcester

1861

1 October — Francis Thomas (Frank) Elgar born

1864	Begins to learn the piano
1 January	Helen Agnes (Dot) Elgar born
5 May	Henry John Elgar dies of scarlet fever
1866	
7 September	Frederick Joseph dies of scarlet fever
10 September	Attends his first Three Choirs Festival rehearsal
1867	Writes first dated music. Schooling continues at Spetchley Park
1868	Attends Littleton House school
1869	Attends the Three Choirs Festival (Worcester). Starts to play the violin
1870	Plays violin at the Crown Hotel Glee Club
1872	
29 May	Completes *The Language of Flowers*, his first song, which he dedicates to his sister Lucy on her 20th birthday
26 June	Finishes at Littleton House. Apprenticed to the solicitor, William Allen, in Worcester
14 July	Plays the organ for Mass at St. George's Church for the first time
1873	
31 January	Sings in a concert at the Union Workhouse
18 April	Attends a Philharmonic Concert at Hereford
June	Leaves Allen's office. Arranges a *Credo* on themes by Beethoven

1875

13 November	Plays in the orchestra (2nd violin) when the Worcester Musical Society gives Spohr's *The Last Judgement*
December	Plays in Handel's *Messiah*

1876

16 May	Plays (1st violin) in Mendelssohn's *Elijah*. Begins teaching the violin
16 September	*Salve Regina* for St.George's Church
23 October	Arranges Wagner's overture to *The Flying Dutchman* for Glee Club ensemble
22 November	Plays (1st violin) in Haydn's *The Seasons*
27 November	*Tantum Ergo* for St. George's Church

1877

12 January	Plays (1st violin) in Barnett's *Paradise and the Peri*
16 March	*Reminiscences* for violin and piano
August	Has violin lessons with Adolph Pollitzer in London. Also begins to play the bassoon in a woodwind quintet with brother Frank (oboe), Hubert Leicester (flute), William Leicester (clarinet) and Frank Exton (flute)
Christmas	Writes *Peckham March* for the quintet

1878

4 April	Completes *Harmony Music* (later renamed *Shed*)
May	Writes the *Evesham Variations* and *Harmony Music* or *Shed No. 2*. Starts *Shed No. 3* but later abandons it. Continues lessons with Pollitzer who introduces Elgar to August Manns and the Crystal Palace concerts. Starts to write *Promenades* for the quintet

21 July	Writes a hymn for St. George's Church
August	Sketches part of a symphony in G minor
September	Plays (2nd violin) in orchestra at Three Choirs Festival
17 September	Completes *Shed No. 4* for the quintet
1 October	Begins to sketch the Minuet of his symphony
November	Hears Hans von Bülow play Schumann's *Fantasy Pieces* in London
21 December	Scores a Minuet in B flat for an ensemble at Powick County Lunatic Asylum

1879

January	Appointed musical director at Powick and writes dance music for the band
7 March	Starts a *Polonaise for Violin and Piano*
23 April	Pollie Elgar marries William Grafton
21 June	*Tantum ergo* and *Domine salvum fac* (completed Spring 1879) given first performances at 50th anniversary of St. George's Church
11 September	Completes a set of Quadrilles for Powick

1880

14 February	Completes a set of *Valentine Lancers* for Powick
15 August	Charles Pipe (Elgar's future brother-in-law) received into the Catholic Church
17–23 August	Visits Paris with Charles Pipe
October	Writes a set of quadrilles (*Paris*) for Powick

1881

February	Hears Mendelssohn's *Hebrides* Overture and E-minor String Quartet in London

17 May	*Air de Ballet* performed by the Worcester Amateur Instrumental Society
September	Plays (1st violin) in orchestra at Three Choirs Festival and hears Alexander Mackenzie's cantata *The Bride*
14 September	Commences *Pas redoublé* No. 2
October	Visits London and hears works by Berlioz, one conducted by Hans Richter, at St. James's Hall

1882

20 February	*March Pas redoublé* played at a Worcester Amateur Instrumental Society concert
17 April	Attempts to write a setting of *O Salutaris Hostia* for solo bass
30 April	Sketches a study for violin
7 May	Sketches a *Benedictus* with nearly complete string parts
August	Sketches a trio for violin, cello and piano. Meets Charles Buck (through John Beare) at Worcester conference of the B.M.A. and spends a holiday with him in Settle, Yorkshire
15 October	Writes a *Polka*, dedicated to Helen Weaver
31 December	Travels to Leipzig and Helen Weaver

1883

14 January	Hears Wagner's *Tannhaüser*
3 March	Attends a Wagner Memorial Concert Crystal Palace
4 April	*Intermezzo moresque* given its first performance in Worcester
May	Attends first English performance of Berlioz's *Requiem* at Crystal Palace

Summer	Moves to home of Charles and Lucy Pipe. Engaged to Helen Weaver
1 October	Finishes another *Polka* ('Helcia') for Powick
13 December	*Intermezzo moresque* played in Birmingham

1884

1 May	*Sevillana* played by the Worcester Philharmonic Society
12 May	*Sevillana* conducted by Manns at Crystal Palace. Attends the first English performance of Brahms's 3rd Symphony, Richter conducting
July	Engagement to Helen Weaver broken off
August	Visits Scotland
September	Dvorak conducts his *Stabat Mater* and Symphony No. 6 at Worcester with Elgar in the orchestra
October	Resigns Bandmaster's post at Powick. Negotiates the publication of a *Romance in E minor* for violin and piano with Schott in London; becomes Opus 1

1885

February	*Sevillana* played in Birmingham at a Stockley concert. Proposes to write a 'Scottish' Overture
10 August	Schott publish a *Gavotte* for violin and piano which is dedicated to Charles Buck
8 October	Plays in performance of work by Frederick Bridge and Stanford's *The Three Holy Innocents*

1886

January	Takes over as organist at St. George's Church, Worcester
10 April	Attends a Crystal Palace concert in honour of the 75 year old Franz Liszt

August	Works on a Trio for violin, cello and piano
6 October	Caroline Alice Roberts (b. 9 October 1848) has first violin lesson with Elgar

1887

27 January	Sketches a choral setting of the *Pie Jesu* in memory of William Allen, the Worcester solicitor
24 February	Plays in the first Birmingham performance of Verdi's *Requiem*
March	*Thro' the long days* (written in 1885) published by Stanley Lucas
25 May	Attends Richter concert and hears Brahms's *Academic Festival Overture* and Bruckner's 7th Symphony
1 July	Sketches a setting of the Lute Song from Tennyson's 'Queen Mary'
September	Plays at Worcester Festival in the first performance of Cowen's oratorio *Ruth*. Starts ladies' orchestral class
1 November	Sketches a Sonata for violin and piano

1888

23 February	Stockley's orchestra performs Elgar's *Suite* with Elgar conducting
7 May	A *Suite for Strings* is performed at a Worcester Musical Union concert
July	A setting of Alice Roberts's poem – *The Wind at Dawn* – appears in the Magazine of Music because it had won a prize in the publisher's competition. Also finishes *Liebesgrüss* (Love's Greeting), later re-titled *Salut d'amour*
22 September	Engaged to Alice Roberts

9 October	*Ecce Sacerdos Magnus* performed during a visit of the Archbishop of Birmingham to St. George's Church
December	Contract signed with Schott to publish *Salut d'amour*

1889

January	Writes a two-movement Sonatina for piano
17 April	Goes to London and makes the arrangements for his wedding
8 May	Married at the Brompton Oratory
28 May	Returns to London from their honeymoon on the Isle of Wight
24 June	Attends an all-Wagner concert, conducted by Richter
July	Attends three performances of *Die Meistersinger* at Covent Garden
29 August	Sketches *The Black Knight*
13 September	Sends the final version of *Queen Mary's Song* to Orsborn and Tuckwood
10 October	Moves into Oaklands, Upper Norwood
26 October	Hears Mendelssohn's overture *Calm Sea and Prosperous Voyage* at Crystal Palace
11 November	Hears August Mann conduct *Salut d'amour* in an afternoon concert at Crystal Palace
21 December	Announced (in the *Daily Telegraph*) that Elgar would write a work for the 1890 Three Choirs Festival at Worcester

1890

1-2 January	*Vesper Voluntaries* for organ completed and sold to Orsborn and Tuckwood
13 January	Leaves some part-songs at Novello & Co., one of which is accepted for publication: *My Love Dwelt in a Northern Land*

20 February	His orchestral *Suite* performed at Crystal Palace
6 April	Note in his diary: 'Begins Overture for Worcester'
25 May	Note in diary : 'Commenced *Froissart*'
27 July	*Froissart* completed and offered to Novello & Co. for publication
8 August	Novello & Co. accepts publication
14 August	Daughter, Carice Irene, born
10 September	*Froissart* first performed at Worcester, conducted by Elgar
November	Begins weekly visits to Worcester to give violin lessons

1891

24 January	'Thinking of leaving London' (Diary)
5 February	*Froissart* performed in Birmingham
14 April	Plays in a performance of Hubert Parry's oratorio *Judith*
May	House-hunting around Malvern
15 June	Leaves London and moves to Malvern
December	Buys a Gagliano violin

1892

31 March	Starts to write *Serenade for Strings*
April	Starts to write *The Black Knight*
23 July	Delivers vocal score to Novello & Co.
28 July	Hears Wagner's *Parsifal* at Bayreuth
1 August	Attends another performance of *Parsifal*
30 September	Completed vocal and piano score of *The Black Knight* sent to Novello & Co.

1893

Spring	Takes up golf
18 April	Premiere of *The Black Knight*
2 August	Travels to Bavaria for a holiday. Hears more operas by Wagner
September	Plays violin in Three Choirs Festival for the last time

1894

8 April	Completes *Sursum Corda*
June	Arranges *Parsifal* Good Friday Music for Worcester High School
July	Begins to compose *King Olaf*
21 July	Alice Elgar received into the Roman Catholic Church
31 July	Travel to Bavaria for a holiday
November	Orchestrates Hugh Blair's *Advent Cantata*

1895

February-April	Works on *Scenes from the Bavarian Highlands*
April	Composes an Organ Sonata
8 July	Première of Organ Sonata
August	Holiday in Bavaria
Autumn	Works on *King Olaf*. Three Choirs Festival commission a short oratorio

1896

February	Vocal scores of both *King Olaf* and *The Light of Life* completed
21 April	*Scenes from the Bavarian Highlands* first performed by Worcester Festival Chorus

8 September	*The Light of Life* first performed at the Worcester Three Choirs Festival
30 October	*King Olaf* first performed at the North Staffordshire Festival, Hanley
November	Commissions from Novello for *Imperial March* and *The Banner of St. George*

1897

January–February	Composes *The Banner of St. George*
15 March	Completes *The Banner of St. George*
19 April	*Imperial March* performed at Crystal Palace
18 May	*The Banner of St. George* performed in London
15 June	Completes a *Te Deum* and *Benedictus* for the Hereford Festival. Begins correspondence with A.J. Jaeger
10 August	Visits Garmisch and Munich
November	Receives commission from Leeds for *Caractacus*

1898

12 June	Vocal score of *Caractacus* completed
September	Idea for 'Gordon' symphony for the 1899 Three Choirs Festival
5 October	Première of *Caractacus* at Leeds
21 October	Begins the *'Enigma'* Variations

1899

5–19 February	Scores the Variations. Sent to Richter for consideration
24 May	*To her Beneath whose Steadfast Star* performed at Windsor Castle in celebration of Queen Victoria's 80th birthday

21 June	Première of 'Enigma' Variations under Richter at St James's Hall
31 July	Extension of the 'Enigma' finale completed
13 September	Revised version of The Light of Life performed at Worcester Three Choirs Festival
5 October	Première of Sea Pictures at the Norwich Festival

1900

23 January	Decides to write The Dream of Gerontius for a Birmingham Festival commission
11 June	Swinnerton Heap, chorus master for the Birmingham Festival dies
3 August	The full score of Gerontius completed
5 October	Première of Gerontius given at Birmingham
22 November	Receives a doctorate at the University of Cambridge

1901

22 January	Death of Queen Victoria
12 March	Receives verses, by Binyon, for a Coronation Ode
20 June	Cockaigne given its first performance at Queen's Hall, London
June–July	Orchestrates Emmaus for Herbert Brewer
19 October	Pomp and Circumstance Marches Nos. 1 and 2 played for the first time in Liverpool
21 October	Grania and Diarmid music performed at Gaiety Theatre, Dublin
2 December	Concert Allegro for piano first performed at St James's Hall, London
19 December	Gerontius performed in Dusseldorf under Buths

1902

31 March	Vocal score of *Coronation Ode* completed
20 May	Second performance of *Gerontius* in Dusseldorf. Richard Strauss toasts Elgar.
26 June	Coronation postponed because of King Edward VII's illness. Affects performance of the *Coronation Ode*. Begins collecting material for *The Apostles*
9 August	Coronation of Edward VII takes place. Takes holiday in Germany
1 September	Death of Ann Elgar
11 September	Expurgated version of *Gerontius* given at Worcester Festival
2 October	*Coronation Ode* given its first performance at Sheffield
October–December	Begins work on *The Apostles*

1903

Spring	Changes of plan over *The Apostles*
6 June	First London performance of *Gerontius* in Westminster Cathedral
25 June	*Coronation Ode* performed in the Royal Albert Hall in presence of King and Queen
17 August	*The Apostles* completed in full score
14 October	Première of *The Apostles* at Birmingham. Elgar Festival planned at Covent Garden
9 November	Death of Alfred Rodewald
21 November	Leaves for Italy. Decides to write *In the South* for the Elgar Festival

1904

3 February	Returns to London and dines with the King and the Prince of Wales
21 February	Completes *In the South*
14–16 March	Elgar festival, with première of *In the South* on 16 March
22 June	Receives degree at the University of Durham
24 June	Knighthood announced
30 June	Moves to Plâs Gwyn, Hereford
26 November	Accepts offer of professorship at the University of Birmingham
28 November	Leaves for Continental trip with Schuster

1905

7 February	Receives honorary doctorate at the University of Oxford, arranged by Hubert Parry
8 March	*Introduction and Allegro* and *Pomp and Circumstance No. 3* given their first performances at Queen's Hall in London
16 March	Gives Inaugural lecture at Birmingham
9 June	Leaves for the USA
28 June	Receives an honorary doctorate at Yale
11 July	Returns to England
12 September	Receives the Freedom of the City of Worcester, arranged through Hubert Leicester as mayor
15 September	Leaves for Mediterranean cruise
25 September	Visits Istanbul
30 September	Visits Smyrna

12 October	Returns to England
December	Starts work on *The Kingdom*

1906

27 March	Completes Scenes I–III of *The Kingdom*
6 April	Leaves for the USA
17 April	Arrives in Cincinnati
May	Scoring of *The Apostles* begun
18 May	Starts return journey to England
31 August	Score of *The Apostles* completed
26 September	Receives honorary doctorate at the University of Aberdeen
3 October	Première of *The Apostles* at Birmingham
28 December	Leaves for Naples

1907

January	Visits Naples and Capri
23 February	Returns to England
2 March	Leaves for the USA
27 April	Returns to Hereford
2 June	Celebrates his 50th birthday
7 June	Completes *Pomp and Circumstance* No.4
July	Completes the *Wand of Youth* suite No.1
24 August	*Pomp and Circumstance* No.4 given its première
5 November	Departs for Rome
3 December	Finally decides to give up the idea of a third oratorio on the Apostles. Starts to compose *Symphony No. 1*

14 December	Première of the *Wand of Youth* suite No. 1 at Queen's Hall

1908

13 January	William Grafton dies
8 May	Leaves for Rome
29 May	Returns to Hereford
Summer	Resumes work on the Symphony
14 August	Attends Elgar concert in Ostend
29 August	Resigns Birmingham professorship
9 September	Première of *Wand of Youth* Suite No.2 at Worcester Three Choirs Festival
25 September	*Symphony No. 1* completed
3 December	Première of the Symphony in Manchester under Richter
7 December	London première of the Symphony

1909

Spring	Affected by much ill-health and depression
22 April	Arrives in Careggi, near Florence. Sketches *Violin Concerto* and *Symphony No 2*
18 May	Jaeger dies
22 June	Returns to Hereford
24 September	First meeting of a Musical League for Composers in Liverpool. Accepts the Presidency

1910

January	Works on the *Violin Concerto* and a *Romance* for bassoon
24 January	Jaeger memorial concert

February	Alice Stuart Wortley becomes the 'Windflower'
7 March	Moves to 58 Cavendish Street
March–April	Motor tour with Frank Schuster to Cornwall
7 May	Death of King Edward VII
28 May	W.H.Reed to help with the *Violin Concerto*
18 June	Returns to Plâs Gwyn
5 August	Completes the orchestration of the *Violin Concerto*
10 November	Première of the *Violin Concerto* with Kreisler as soloist

1911

16 February	Première of the bassoon *Romance* in Hereford
28 February	Completes *Symphony No. 2*
25 March	Leaves for tour of North America
9 May	Returns to Hereford
23 May	*Symphony No. 2* given its first performance
20 June	Awarded the Order of Merit. Attends rehearsals in Westminster Abbey for the Coronation Service
22 June	*Coronation March* and *O Hearken Thou* performed at the Coronation Service which the Elgars do not attend
14 September	Elgar/Atkins edition of the Bach *Matthew Passion* performed at Worcester Festival

1912

1 January	Moves to Severn House, Hampstead
11 March	*The Crown of India* first performed
16 July	*Psalm 48* performed in Westminster Abbey
20 August	Completes *The Music Makers*

1 October	Première of *The Music Makers* in Birmingham

1913

31 January	Leaves for Naples
8 February	Arrives in Naples
23 February	Returns to Severn House
22 March	Begins work on *Falstaff*
9 June	Julia Worthington dies
20 July	Chaliapin visits Severn House. Mention of *King Lear* as an opera
5 August	Completes *Falstaff*
1 October	Première of *Falstaff* at Leeds
December	Sends sketch of a piano concerto to the Windflower

1914

20 January	Records *Carissima* for the Gramophone Company
2 March	Signs pledge against Irish Home Rule
18 May	Celebrates his Silver wedding
19 July	Takes a holiday in Scotland
4 August	World War I starts
14 August	Returns to Severn House
17 August	Volunteers as a Special Constable
7 December	Premiere of *Carillon*

1915

January	Receives proposal for a setting of Binyon poems
Spring	Completes *For the Fallen*
6 July	Première of *Polonia*

September	Holiday with the Stuart Wortleys near Ravenglass
November	Composes *The Starlight Express*
29 December	Première of *The Starlight Express*

1916

29 January	Première of *Une voix dans le désert*
18 February	Records *The Starlight Express*
8 April	Taken ill on a train journey to Stoke Prior
3 May	Première of *To Women* and *For the Fallen*
August	Holiday in the Lake District

1917

20 March	Première of *The Sanguine Fan*
14 April	Première of *Le drapeau belge*
11 June	Première of *The Fringes of the Fleet*
24 May	First stay at Brinkwells
24 November	Première of the complete *Spirit of England*

1918

15 March	Tonsils removed
2 May	Move to Brinkwells. Starts work on the *Cello Concerto* and a String Quartet
20 August	Starts work on a *Violin Sonata*
15 September	Completes the *Violin Sonata*
26 September	Starts work on a *Piano Quintet*, and from 9 October, works simultaneously on it and the *String Quartet*
29 October	Lady Elgar has an operation for a wen
11 November	World War I ends

24 December	*String Quartet* completed

1919

9 February	*Piano Quintet* completed
7 March	Three chamber works performed at Severn House in the presence of Arthur Bliss and G.B.Shaw
21 May	Public première of the chamber works
8 August	*Cello Concerto* completed
27 October	Première of *Cello Concerto* with Felix Salmond

1920

7 April	Lady Elgar dies at 6.10pm
10 April	Buried at St Wulstan's Church, Little Malvern
1– 23 October	Visits Amsterdam and Brussels with Carice
10 November	Conducts an all Elgar programme at the first concert by the City of Birmingham Orchestra
November	Heifetz visits Severn House

1921

23 March	Carice Elgar engaged to Samuel Blake
25 May	Orchestration of the Bach Organ Fugue completed
27 October	Première of the Bach *Fugue in C minor*
November	Severn House sold: move to 37 St. James's Place
December	Invites Bliss and Goossens to write works for the 1922 Gloucester Festival

1922

16 January	Marriage of Carice Elgar
7 September	Première of Bach-Elgar *Fantasia and Fugue in C minor* at Gloucester Three Choirs Festival

1923

February	Finishes music for Binyon's *Arthur*
12 March	Première of music for *Arthur*
31 March	Moves to Napleton Grange, Kempsey
2 September	Première of the Handel-Elgar *Overture in D minor* at the Worcester Three Choirs Festival
15 November	Departs for South America and a cruise up the River Amazon on RMS Hildebrand
30 December	Returns to England

1924

28 April	Appointed Master of the King's Music
21 July	Première of *Empire March* and songs for *Pageant of Empire*

1925

Spring	Resigns from the Athenaeum Club
23 October	Lucy Pipe dies

1926

24 April	Lord Stuart of Wortley dies

1927

26 February	Makes a part recording of *Gerontius* at the Royal Albert Hall
2 June	Celebrates his 70th birthday and conducts a birthday concert for the BBC
26 June	Schuster gives a concert of the chamber works
4 September	Première of *A Civic Fanfare* at the Hereford Three Choirs Festival

27 December	Death of Schuster who leaves Elgar £7000

1928

1 January	Appointed K.C.V.O. in the New Year's Honours
Spring	Moves to Tiddington House, Stratford
7 June	Frank Elgar dies
5 November	Première of *Beau Brummell* music

1929

17 August	Opens a Shaw exhibition at the Malvern Festival
6 November	Records *Improvisations*
9 December	Première of *Good Morrow* at Windsor Castle

1930

16 April	*Severn Suite* completed and dedicated to George Bernard Shaw
18 September	*Pomp and Circumstance* No. 5 given its first performance
27 September	*Severn Suite* given its first performance
December	Completes the *Nursery Suite*

1931

3 June	Becomes First Baronet of Broadheath
7 November	Meets Vera Hockman
12 November	Opens HMV recording studios in Abbey Road, London

1932

March	Orchestrates *Funeral March* from Chopin's B flat minor Piano Sonata

April	*Severn Suite* scored for full orchestra
June	Discusses proposal for *Third Symphony* with Keith Prowse
14–15 July	Records the *Violin Concerto* with Menuhin
September	Approaches Barry Jackson for help over the libretto for his opera *The Spanish Lady*
December	Three BBC concerts to celebrate his 75th birthday, with an announcement on 14 December that the BBC was commissioning the *Third Symphony*

1933

Spring	Works on the opera and the symphony
28 May	Flies to Paris for a performance of the *Violin Concerto* with Menuhin. Visits Delius at Grez
3 June	Created K.C.V.O.
6 September	Viola version of the *Cello Concerto* performed at the Hereford Three Choirs Festival
October	Enters South Bank nursing home. Correspondence with Delius

1934

3 January	Returns to Marl Bank
22 January	Listens to recording session of Triumphal March from *Caractacus* and asks for the 'Woodland Interlude'
15 February	Criticises the recording of *Mina*
23 February	Dies at 7.45am
26 February	Buried at Little Malvern

Catalogue Raisonné

1866

'BACH' Motif
Dated 24 March 1866

1867

Humoreske
(A Tune from Broadheath)

1869

Fugue in G minor
for organ (unfinished)
Reproduced in *The Music Student*, August 1916, p. 346

1872

Chantant
for solo piano

The Language of Flowers
Song for voice and piano
Text: James G. Percival (1795–1856)
'To my sister Lucy on her birthday'

1873

Credo on Themes from Symphonies 5, 7 and 9 by Beethoven
Arranged by 'Bernhard Pappenheim' (E.E.) for soloists, mixed
chorus and organ
Text: The Ordinary of the Mass
First performance: Worcester, St. George's Church, 1873

1874

Anthem with original introduction
Arranged for mixed chorus, strings and organ
First performance: Worcester, All Saint's Church, 1874

1875

Arrangements of 'Christmas Pieces'
for flute and string quartet of works by Beethoven, Boccherini,
Chopin, Gluck, Handel and Mendelssohn.
Also includes arrangements for *Adeste Fidelis* by the composer

The Self Banished
Song for voice and piano
Text: Edmund Waller (1607–1687)

Two movements for oboe and string quartet in G
1. Andante sostenuto
2. Allegro

1875–76

Various Arrangements of Fugues etc.
for string quartet of works by Bach, Beethoven, Geissler, Handel, Hesse,
Mendelssohn, Mozart, Rinck and Spohr

1876

Imitation a Quattro Through all the Parts Alternately
After the 2nd movement of Beethoven's *Violin Sonata in* G (Op.30)
for string quartet

Salve Regina
for mixed chorus and organ
Text: Antiphon at Compline
First performance: Worcester, St. George's Church, 6 June 1880.
Resident choir with William Elgar (organ), directed by Edward Elgar

Tantum Ergo
for mixed chorus and organ
Text: Hymn at Communion
First performance: Worcester, St. George's Church, 29 June 1879.
Resident choir with William Elgar (organ), directed by Edward Elgar

1877

Adagio in C
for solo violin

Arpeggio Studies in E and A
for solo violin

Credo in E
for mixed chorus and organ
Text: The Ordinary of the Mass

Peckham March
for wind quintet
2 flutes, oboe, clarinet and bassoon
'Edward Elgar'

Reminiscences
for violin and piano
'Oswin Grainger'

1878

Adagio
from the 2nd movement of Spohr's *Duet for two violins*, Op.39,
arranged for two violins and [cello] (fragment)

Adagio Cantabile: 'Mrs Winslow's Soothing Syrup'
for wind quintet
2 flutes, oboe, clarinet and bassoon
Belwin-Mills Music, 1976

Adeste Fidelis
arranged for wind quartet
Flute, oboe, clarinet and bassoon

Allegro in Bb
for oboe, violin, viola and cello
Incomplete

Allegro Molto
from the 3rd movement of Beethoven's *Sonata for Violin and Piano*, Opus 23
arranged for wind quintet
2 flutes, oboe, clarinet and bassoon

Andante con variazione (Evesham andante)
for wind quintet
2 flutes, oboe, clarinet and bassoon
'H.A.L.' [Hubert Leicester]
Belwin-Mills Music, 1976

Andante in G
for 2 flutes, 2 oboes, 2 clarinets, [bassoon and strings]
Incomplete

Andante Largo from Corelli's Concerto Grosso Op. 6 no. 10
Arranged for 2 flutes, 2 oboes, 2 clarinets, 2 bassoons and strings

Archer's Song
arranged for voice, piano and violin
'Oswin Grainger'

Dead March from Handel's 'Saul'
Arranged for cornet and organ
Incomplete

Etude Caprice
for solo violin

Exercise for the Third Finger
for solo violin
Revised in 1920 for Jascha Heifetz as
Study for Strengthening the Third Finger

Fantasia
for violin and piano
Incomplete

Harmony Music No. 1 (Shed No. 1)
for wind quintet
2 flutes, oboe, clarinet and bassoon
'Professor Exton'
Belwin-Mills Music, 1976

Harmony Music No. 2 'Nelly Shed' (Shed No. 2)
for wind quintet
2 flutes, oboe, clarinet and bassoon
'W. Leicester'
Belwin-Mills Music, 1976

Harmony Music No. 3: 'Nelly Shed' (Shed No. 3)
for wind quintet
2 flutes, oboe, clarinet and bassoon
'Frank Elgar'
Belwin-Mills Music, 1976

Harmony Music No. 4 : 'The Farm Yard' (Shed No. 4)
for wind quintet
2 flutes, oboe, clarinet and bassoon
Belwin-Mills Music, 1976

Hymn Tune in C major
for SATB
Published as No. 63 'Praise ye the Lord; on ev'ry height'
in a collection for St. George's Church, Worcester (1878)

Hymn Tune in F major ('Drakes Broughton')
for SATB
Published as No 151 'Hear Thy children, gentle Jesus'
in the Westminster Hymnal, 1898 and 1912

Hymn Tune in G major
for SATB
Published as No. 89 'Now with the fast-departing light'
in a collection for St. George's Church, Worcester (1878)

Intonation No.2
for 2 flutes, 2 oboes, 2 clarinets and strings

Introductory Overture for Christy Minstrels
for flute, cornet, percussion and strings
First performance: Worcester, the Music Hall, 12 June 1878

Kyrie in C
for mixed chorus and organ
Text: The Ordinary of the Mass
Incomplete

Largo Cantabile: Theme and Variations
for wind quintet
2 flutes, oboe, clarinet and bassoon
Incomplete

Magnificat in F
for mixed chorus and organ
Text: The Latin Vulgate
Incomplete

Magnificat in G
Text: The Latin Vulgate
Incomplete

Menuetto from Mozart's Symphony No.39 (K.543)
Arranged in D major
2 flutes, 2 oboes, clarinet, cornet and strings

Menuetto in Bb
for wind quintet
2 flutes, oboe, clarinet and bassoon
Belwin-Mills Music, 1977

Oh! 'tis a glorious sight
Recitative and Aria from Weber's 'Oberon' (Act II)
arranged for tenor solo and strings

Overture to Handel's 'Ariodante'
Third movement arranged for 2 oboes and strings

Promenade No. 1
for wind quintet
2 flutes, oboe, clarinet and bassoon
Belwin-Mills Music, 1976

Promenade No. 2: Mme Taussaud's [sic]
for wind quintet
2 flutes, oboe, clarinet and bassoon
Belwin-Mills Music, 1976

Promenade No. 3
for wind quintet
2 flutes, oboe, clarinet and bassoon
Belwin-Mills Music, 1976

Promenade No. 4: 'Somniferous'
for wind quintet
2 flutes, oboe, clarinet and bassoon
Belwin-Mills Music, 1976

Promenade No. 5: 'Skip'
for wind quintet
2 flutes, oboe, clarinet and bassoon
Belwin-Mills Music, 1976

Promenade No. 6: 'Hell and Tommy'
for wind quintet
2 flutes, oboe, clarinet and bassoon
Belwin-Mills Music, 1976

Quartet for Strings in Bb
Incomplete

Quartet for Strings in D minor
Incomplete

Romance (Op.1)
for violin and piano
'Oswin Grainger'
First performance: Worcester, The Deanery, 20 October 1885
Schott, 1885

Rondeau – Temple Bar
Song for tenor and piano
Incomplete

Solemn March
from March in C by I.X. Leybach
arranged for wind quintet
2 flutes, oboe, clarinet and bassoon

Sonata in C
for [violin] and piano (fragment)

Symphony in G minor after Mozart (K550)
1.2.2.2/4.0.0.0/timp. (2)/strings
Incomplete

Trio Movement in C
for two violins and cello (fragment)

1879

Andantino in G
for flute, oboe, clarinet, 2 horns and strings (fragment)

Ballet Music
1. Ensemble
2. Moderato
3. Allegro
Flute, oboe, clarinet, bassoon and strings (fragment)

Brother, For Thee He Died
Easter anthem for solo voice and piano
Incomplete

Domine salvam fac reginam nostram victoriam
Motet for mixed chorus, flute, oboe, organ and strings
Text: A Prayer for the Queen
First performance: Worcester, St. George's Church, 29 June 1879

Five Intermezzi
for wind quintet
1. 'Nancy' (Allegretto)
2. 'Mrs & Miss Howells' (Adagio solenne)
3. 'The Farm Yard' (Allegro molto)
4. Andante con moto
5. Allegretto, No 2
2 flutes, oboe, clarinet and bassoon
Belwin-Mills Music, 1977

Five Quadrilles – L'Assommoir
Piccolo, flute, clarinet, 2 cornets, euphonium, strings and piano

Five Quadrilles – La Brunette
Piccolo, flute, clarinet, 2 cornets, euphonium, strings and piano
'George Jenkins' [Clerk at the Powick Lunatic Asylum]

Five Quadrilles or Caledonians, Die Junge Kokette
Piccolo, flute, clarinet, 2 cornets, euphonium, strings and piano
'Miss J Holloway' [Pianist and organist]

Gavotte ('The Alphonsa')
for wind quintet
2 flutes, oboe, clarinet and bassoon
Belwin-Mills Music, 1977

Gigue-allegretto
for wind quintet
2 flutes, oboe, clarinet and bassoon

Harmony Music No. 5 (Shed No.5)
for wind quintet
1. 'The Mission' (Allegro moderato)
2. Minuetto and Trio
3. 'Noah's Ark' (Andante)
4. Finale
2 flutes, oboe, clarinet and bassoon
Belwin-Mills Music, 1977

Harmony Music No. 6 (Shed No.6)
for wind quintet
1. Allegro molto
2. Andante arioso
3. Menuet and trio
4. Finale
2 flutes, oboe, clarinet and bassoon

Andante arioso arranged and revised in 1912 as
Cantique (Op.3) for orchestra, organ or piano
'Hugh Blair'
First performance: London, Royal Albert Hall, 15 December 1912.
New Symphony Orchestra, conducted by Landon Ronald
Novello, 1913 (organ arrangement)

National Anthem
arranged for solo piano (in D)

Orchestration of 'Ognor più Tenero' from Carafa's 'Masaniello'
Solo flute + 2.2.2.2/2.0.1.0/timp.(2)/strings
'Frank Hadley'
The full score is dated 1 May 1879, but does not include parts for 2 flutes, 2 horns or trombone. These were added later and appear in the parts, together with an original introduction (18 bars) composed by Elgar.

Polonaise in D minor
for violin and piano (incomplete)
First performance: Doncaster, 15 May 1974.
Paul Collins (violin) and John Parry (piano)

Polonaise in F
for violin and piano (incomplete)
'For J.H. [Miss J Holloway] with esteem'
First performance: Doncaster, 15 May 1974
Paul Collins (violin) and John Parry (piano)

Sarabande-Largo
for wind quintet
2 flutes, oboe, clarinet and bassoon
Belwin-Mills Music, 1977

Study in A
for solo violin

Trio in C
for flute, oboe and [clarinet]
Allegro
Adagio
[Rondo]

1880

Five Lancers ('The Valentine')
Piccolo, flute, clarinet, 2 cornets, euphonium, strings and piano

Five Quadrilles – 'Paris'
1. Châtelet
2. L'Hippodrome
3. Alcazar d'Été (Champs Elysees)
4. Là! Suzanne
5. Café des ambassadeurs: La femme d'emballeur
Piccolo, flute, clarinet, 2 cornets, euphonium, strings and piano
'Miss J. Holloway'

Gloria
Allegro from Mozart's *Sonata in F for violin and piano*, K.547,
arranged as a Gloria for soli, mixed chorus and organ
First performance: Worcester, St. George's Church

O Salutaris Hostia in Eb
for mixed chorus and organ
Text: Gregorian Hymn
'To my father – with affection'
Cary, 1888

O Salutaris Hostia in F
for mixed chorus and organ
Text: Gregorian Hymn
Cary, [1898]

Polka – 'Maud'
Piccolo, flute, clarinet, 2 cornets, euphonium, strings and piano

1881

Air de Ballet
for orchestra
2.1.1.0/2.0.0 euph./timp. perc./strings
First performance: Worcester, 17 May 1881.
The Worcester Amateur Instrumental Society Orchestra, conducted by
A.J. Caldicott
Arrangement for piano solo by Gustave Franke (alias Frank Elgar)
under the title *Pastorelle*
Boosey, 1903

Andante and Air
for oboe [and piano]
Incomplete

Fantasia on Irish Airs
for violin and piano
Incomplete

Harmony Music No. 7 (Shed No.7)
for wind quintet
1. Allegro
2. Allegro giusto
2 flutes, oboe, clarinet and bassoon

March – Pas Redoublé (No. 1)
for orchestra
First performance: Worcester, the Glee Club, 1 March 1881

Polka ('Nelly')
Piccolo, flute, clarinet, 2 cornets, euphonium, strings and piano
'Helen Weaver'

Study in D
for solo violin

1882

Benedictus sit Deus Pater
Offertory for mixed chorus, strings and organ
Text: Offertory in Festo Ss.Trinitatis
Incomplete

March – Pas Redoublé (No. 2)
for orchestra
First performance: Worcester, Guildhall, 20 February 1882.
The Worcester Amateur Instrumental Society Orchestra, conducted
by A.J. Caldicott

Menuetto and Trio in G
for violin, cello and piano

Revised and arranged for orchestra in 1915 as
Rosemary
2.1.2.2/2.2 corn.3.0/timp./perc./harp/strings
Elkin, 1915

Polka ('La Blonde')
Piccolo, flute, clarinet, 2 cornets, euphonium, strings and piano
'Helen Weaver'

O Salutaris Hostia
arranged for voice and piano
Text: Gregorian hymn

1883

Entry of the Minstrels from Wagner's 'Tannhäuser'
arranged for solo piano

Fugue in D minor
for oboe and violin
'Frank Elgar and Karl Bammert'

Intermezzo Moresque
for orchestra
First performance: Birmingham, Town Hall, 13 December 1883.
Stockley Orchestra, conducted by W.C. Stockley

Polka ('Helcia')
Piccolo, flute, clarinet, 2 cornets, euphonium, strings and piano

Scherzo from Schumann's 'Overture, Scherzo and Finale' (Op.52)
arranged for solo piano

1884

Griffinesque
for solo piano
Revised in 1885 as *Presto* for piano and dedicated to Mrs Buck
Novello 1981

Pastourelle (Op.4 no.2)
for violin and piano
'Miss Hilda Fitton, Malvern'
Beare, 1885
Novello, 1913

Polka ('Blumine')
Piccolo, flute, clarinet, 2 cornets, euphonium, strings and piano

Scottish Overture
for orchestra (fragment)

A Soldier's Song
Song for voice and piano
Text: C.Flavell Haywood
'F.G.P., Worcester' [F.G.Pedley]
First performance: Worcester, Glee Club (Crown Hotel, Broad Street), 17
March 1884.
F. Pedley (bass)
The Magazine of Music, vol.7 (1890)
Re-named *A War Song* and re-published by Boosey (1903)

Sevillana (Scene Espagnole) (Op. 7)
for orchestra
1+1.2.2.2/4.2 corn.3.0/perc./strings
'W.C. Stockley'
First performance: Worcester, Public Hall, 1 May 1884
Worcestershire Philharmonic Society Orchestra, conducted by W. Done
First London: Crystal Palace, 12 May 1884.
Crystal Palace Orchestra, conducted by August Manns
Revised and rescored in 1889
Tuckwood, 1899 (orchestral score)

Une Idylle (Op.4 no. 1)
for violin and piano
'E.E.(Inverness)'
Beare, 1885
Ashdown, 1910

Virelai (Op.4 no.3)
for violin and piano
'Frank W. Webb'
Beare, 1890
Novello, 1913

1885

Allegretto on G E D G E
for violin and piano
'The Misses Gedge, Malvern'
First performance: Malvern, Wells House, 27 March 1885
Beare, 1885

Cello obbligato to C.H.Dolby's song 'Out on the Rocks'
Song for voice, cello and piano

Cello obbligato to Maud Valerie White's song 'Absent yet Present'
Song for voice, cello and piano

Cello obbligato to Tosti's song 'For Ever and for Ever'
Song for voice' cello and piano

Clapham Town End
Folksong, arranged for voice and piano

Gavotte
for violin and piano
'Dr.C.W.Buck'
Schott, 1886

Harmonisation of vocal melody by C.W. Buck
for voice and piano

A Phylactery
Song for [voice and piano]
Text: John M. Hay (1838–1906)

Through the Long Days (Op.16 no.2)
Song for voice and piano
Text: John M. Hay (1838–1906)
'Rev. E. Vine Hall'
First performance: London, St.James's Hall, 25 February 1897.
Charles Phillips (baritone)
Lucas, 1887
Ascherberg, 1890
Ascherberg, Hopwood & Crew in 'Seven Lieder of Edward Elgar' 1907

1886

Arrangement of G.F. Blackbourne's 'Berceuse Petite Reine'
for violin and piano
Willcocks, 1886

Enina Valse
for solo piano

Four Litanies B.V.M.
for unaccompanied mixed chorus
'Fr. T. Knights, S.J.'
Cary, 1888

Is she not passing fair?
Song for voice and piano
Text: Charles, Duc d'Orleans, tr. L.S. Costello
Boosey, 1908

Stabat Mater
for unaccompanied mixed chorus
Text: J.da Todi (c.1228-1306)

Trio
for violin, cello and piano
Incomplete
First performance: Doncaster, 15 May 1974.
Paul Collins (violin) and John Parry (piano). Unable to trace the cellist

Twenty-seven Litany chants
for unaccompanied mixed chorus
Various published in *Tozer's Benediction Manual*(1898)

1887

As I laye A-thinkynge
Song for soprano or tenor voice and piano
Text: Richard Barham ('Thomas Ingoldsby')
Beare, 1888

Ave Maria gratia plena (Op.2 no.2)
for mixed chorus and organ
Text: Alleluia verse
'Mrs H.A. Leicester'
Novello, 1907 (Latin version, and English version with words by
J.Cummins: *Jesu, Lord of Life and Glory*)

Ave Maria Stella (Op.2 no.3)
for mixed chorus and organ
Text: Marian office hymn
'Rev. Canon Dolman, O.S.B., Hereford'
Novello, 1907 (Latin version, and English version with words by Rev. H.
Collins: *Jesu, Meek and Lowly*)

Ave Verum (Op.2 no.1)
Offertory for mixed chorus and organ
Text:The Offertorium of the *Missa pro Defunctis*
'In memoriam William Allen'
Novello, 1902 as the Gradual *Ave Verum Corpus*
Novello, 1907 with the English text *Jesu, word of God incarnate*

Duett for Trombone and Bass
'O.W. Weaver'

Laura Valse
for solo piano
'Laura Cox'

March
for solo piano

Queen Mary's Song
for voice and piano
Text: Alfred, Lord Tennyson (1809-1892)
'J.H. Meredith' [Honorary member of the Worcester Amateur Instrumental Society]
Orsborn and Tuckwood, 1889
Ascherberg, 1892
Ascherberg, Hopwood & Crew in 'Seven Lieder of Edward Elgar' 1907

Sonata in D (Op.9)
for violin and piano
Incomplete

1888

Ecce sacerdos magnus
Gradual for mixed chorus and organ (or orchestra)
Text: Gradual at Missa de Conessore Pontifice
'Hubert Leicester'
First performance: Worcester, St.George's Church, 9 October 1888
(A special service for the blessing of a statue at the inauguration of a branch of the League of the Apostleship of Prayer by the Bishop of Birmingham.)
Cary, 1888

Laudate Dominum (Chant in Db)
for unison voices and [organ]
Text: Psalm 117

Quartet for Strings in D
Incomplete

Salut d'amour (Liebesgrüss) (Op.12)
for violin and piano
à Carice [Caroline Alice Roberts]
Arranged for orchestra by Elgar
1.2.2.2/2.0.0.0/strings
First performance: London, Crystal Palace, 11 November 1889.
Crystal Palace Orchestra, conducted by August Manns
Schott, 1889

Three Pieces for String Orchestra
1.   Spring Song (Allegro)
2.   Elegy (Adagio)
3.   Finale (Presto)
First performance: Worcester, 7 May 1888.
The Worcestershire Musical Union Orchestra, conducted by Rev. E. Vine Hall
The manuscript of this work was lost: it was probably revised as the *Serenade for String Orchestra* (Op.20)

The Wind at Dawn
Song for voice and piano (orchestrated in 1912 by Elgar)
Text: Caroline Alice Roberts (1848–1920)
'Dr. Ludwig Wüllner'
Magazine of Music, 8 July 1888
Boosey & Hawkes, 1907 (with dedication added)

1889

Bizarrerie (Op.13 no.2)
for violin and piano
Orsborn and Tuckwood, 1890

Mot d'amour (Liebesahnung) (Op.13 no.1)
for violin and piano
'Caroline Alice Elgar'
Orsborn and Tuckwood, 1890

My Love Dwelt in a Northern Land
Part song for mixed voices
Text: Andrew Lang (1844–1912)
'Rev. J. Hampton, M.A., Warden of St. Michael's College, Tenbury'
First performance:Tenbury, Corn Exchange Hall, 13 November 1890.
Tenbury Musical Society, conducted by Rev. J. Hampton
Novello, 1890

O Happy Eyes (Op.18 no.1)
Part song for mixed voices
Text: Caroline Alice Roberts (1848–1920)
Novello, 1896

Presto
for solo piano
'To Miss Isabel Fitton Aug 8; 1889' [her 21st birthday]
Novello, 1981

Sonatina
for solo piano
1.   Andantino
2.   Allegro
'composed expressly for May Grafton by her affectionate Uncle, Edward
Elgar, Jany 4: 1889'
Revised in 1931 and published by Keith Prowse

Vesper Voluntaries (Op.14)
for organ
Introduction
1.   Andante
2.   Allegro
3.   Andantino
4.   Allegretto piacevole Intermezzo
5.   Poco Lento
6.   Moderato
7.   Allegretto pensoso
8.   Poco Allegro
Coda
'Mrs W.A. Raikes'
Orsborn & Tuckwood, 1890

1890

Concerto for Violin and Orchestra (fragment)
Manuscript destroyed during 1890

'Froissart' (Op.19)
Concert Overture for orchestra
Commissioned by the 1890 Three Choirs Festival
2+1.2.2.2+1/4.2.2.0/timp. perc./strings
First performance: Worcester, Public Hall, 10 September 1890
Worcester Festival Orchestra, conducted by Edward Elgar
First London: St. James's Hall, 16 November 1900
Orchestra conducted by Frederic Cowen
Novello, 1901 (Full score)

1891

La Capricieuse – morceau de genre (Op.17)
for violin and piano
'Fred Ward' [a Worcester pupil of Elgar]
Breitkopf and Hartel, 1893

1892

The Black Knight (Op.25)
'Symphony' for mixed chorus and orchestra
Text: L.Uhland, trans. W.H.Longfellow
2+1.2.2.2/4.2.3.0/timp./perc./organ/strings
'To my friend Hugh Blair, M.A., Mus. B'
First performance: Worcester, Public Hall, 18 April 1893
Worcester Festival Choral Society and Orchestra, conducted by Edward Elgar
First London: St.Martin's Town Hall, 28 March 1895
'Miss Holland's Choir' with Miss Holland (piano), conducted by Mr. Prendegast
Novello, 1893

Études Caractéristiques (Op.24)
for solo violin
'Adolphe Pollitzer'
Chanot, 1892

1588: Loose, loose the sails
Song for voice and [piano]
Text: C.A. Elgar (1848–1920)
First performance: Malvern, 'Forli', 26 August 1892
Miss Simpson and Edward Elgar (piano)

The High Tide
Cantata for soli, mixed chorus and orchestra
According to *Michael Kennedy* (1993), Elgar also 'toyed with' the idea of
this work in 1893 and 1901 (for the 1902 Norwich Festival).

Like to the Damask Rose
Song for voice and piano
Text: S. Wastell (1560–1635)
First performance: London, St.James's Hall, 25 February 1897.
Charles Phillips (baritone) and Marie Olsen (piano)
Tuckwood, 1892
Ascherberg, Hopwood & Crew in 'Seven Lieder of Edward Elgar' 1907

The Mill Wheel Songs
1.　Winter
2.　May (a Rhapsody)
Text: C.A. Elgar (1848–1920)

Ophelia's Song (Op.21 no.1)
for voice and piano
Text: William Shakespeare (1564–1616)

The Poet's Life
Song for voice and piano
Text: S. Jewett (1861–1909), alias Ellen Burroughs
Tuckwood, 1892
Ascherberg, Hopwood & Crew in 'Seven Lieder of Edward Elgar' 1907

Serenade in E minor (Op.20)
for string orchestra
1.　Allegro piacevole
2.　Larghetto
3.　Allegretto

'W.H.Winfield'
First performance: Worcester, Ladies' Orchestral Class, May 1892
Ladies' orchestra, conducted by Edward Elgar
First complete performance: Antwerp, 23 July 1896
First complete English performance: New Brighton, 16 July 1899
New Brighton Tower Orchestra, conducted by Edward Elgar
First London: Bechstein Hall, 5 March 1905
London Symphony Orchestra, conducted by Edward Elgar
Breitkopf & Hartel, 1893 (Full score)

The Shepherd's Song (Op.16 no.1)
Song for voice and piano
Text: B.Pain (1864–1928)
Tuckwood, 1895
Ascherberg, Hopwood & Crew in 'Seven Lieder of Edward Elgar' 1907

A Song of Autumn
Song for voice and piano
Text: Adam Lindsay Gordon (1833–1870)
'Miss Marshall'
Tuckwood, 1892
Ascherberg, Hopwood & Crew in 'Seven Lieder of Edward Elgar' 1907

Spanish Serenade (Op.23)
Song for mixed chorus, two violins and piano or orchestra
1.2.2.2/2.0.0.0/timp. perc./strings
Text: H.W. Longfellow (1807–1882)
First performance: Hereford, Shire Hall, 7 April 1893
Herefordshire Philharmonic Society, conducted by Rev. J. Hampton
Novello, 1892

A Spear, a Sword
Song for voice and [piano]
Text: C.A.Elgar (1848–1920)
First performance: Malvern, 'Forli', 28 August 1892.
Miss Simpson and Edward Elgar (piano)

Very Easy Melodious Exercises in the First Position (Op.22)
for violin and piano
'May Grafton' [Elgar's niece]
Chanot, 1892

1893

Offertoire (Andante religioso) (Op.11)
for violin and piano
'Serge Derval'
Boosey, 1903 (under the pseudonym of Gustav Franke)

1894

Good Friday Music from Act III of Wagner's 'Parsifal'
Arranged for 3 violins, cello, 2 pianos and organ
First performance: Worcester, Girls' High School, 13 June 1894.
The Girls' High School Orchestra

Muleteer's Song
Song for voice and piano
Text: C.A. Elgar (1848–1920)

Orchestration of 'Advent Cantata' by Hugh Blair (November 1894)
Cantata for soli(?), chorus and orchestra
First performance: Worcester, Public Hall, 4 December 1894
Worcester Philharmonic Choral Society and Orchestra, conducted by
Hugh Blair

Rondel (Op.16 no.3)
Song for voice and piano
Text: J.Froissart, translated by H. Longfellow
First performance: London, St. James's Hall, 7 December 1897.
Madame Alice Gomez
Tuckwood, 1895
Ascherberg, Hopwood & Crew in 'Seven Lieder of Edward Elgar' 1907

Sursum Corda, Elevation (Op.11)
for 2 trumpets, 4 horns, 3 trombones, tuba, timpani, organ and strings

Written, at the request of Hugh Blair, for a special Cathedral service
honouring a visit to Worcester by the Duke of York, later King George V
'H. Dyke Acland'
First performance: Worcester, Cathedral Church of Christ and St. Mary, 9
April 1894
Orchestra, conducted by Hugh Blair
Schott, 1901

Two Part Songs (Op.26 nos.1 and 2)
for ladies' voices (SAA), 2 violins and piano
1. The Snow
2. Fly, Singing Bird
Text: C.A. Elgar (1848–1920)
'Mrs E.B. Fitton, Malvern'
Novello, 1895
Orchestrated in December 1903
2.2.2.0/2.0.0.0/timp./harp/strings
First performance: London, Queen's Hall, 12 March 1904.

The Wave
Song for voice and piano
Text: C.A. Elgar (1848-1920)

1895

After (Op.31 no.1)
Song for voice and piano
Text: P.B. Marston (1850-1887)
First performance: London, St.James's Hall, 2 March 1900.
H. Plunket Greene (baritone)
Boosey, 1900

Scenes from the Bavarian Highlands (Op.27)
A.   Six choral songs for mixed chorus and piano
1.   The Dance (Sonnenbichel)
2.   False Love (Wamberg)
3.   Lullaby (Im Hammersbach)
4.   Aspiration (Bei Sankt Anton)
5.   On the Alm (Hoch Alp)

6.   The Marksman (Bei Murnau)
Text: Bavarian folksongs, adapted by C.A. Elgar
'Mr & Mrs Henry Slingsby Bethell, Garmisch, Bavaria'
First performance: Worcester, 21 April 1896
Worcester Festival Choral Society, conducted by Edward Elgar
J. Williams, 1896

B.   Three Bavarian Dances for Orchestra (scored 1896)
1.   The Dance (Sonnenbichel)
2.   Lullaby (Im Hammersbach)
3.   The Marksman (Bei Murnau)
2.2.2.2/4.2.2+1.0/timp./perc./strings
First performance: London, Crystal Palace, 23 October 1897.
Crystal Palace Orchestra, conducted by August Manns
J. Williams, 1901

Sonata (Op. 28)
for organ
Written for a visit of American organists to Worcester Cathedral
1.   Allegro maestoso
2.   Allegretto
3.   Andante espressivo
4.   Presto (comodo)
'C. Swinnerton Heap, Mus.D.'
First performance: Worcester, Cathedral Church of Christ and
St. Mary, 8 July 1895.
Hugh Blair (organ)
Breitkopf & Hartel, 1896

A Song of Flight (Op.31 no.2)
Song for voice and piano
Text: C. Rossetti (1820–1894)
First performance: London, St. James's Hall, 2 March 1900.
H.Plunket Greene (baritone)
Boosey, 1900

1896

The Light of Life (Lux Christi) (Op.29)

Oratorio for SATB soli, mixed chorus and orchestra
2.2.2.2+1/2.2.3.1/timp./perc./harp/organ/strings
Text: Rev. E. Capel-Cure (1860–1949)
Commissioned by the 1896 Three Choirs Festival
'C. Swinnerton Heap, Mus.D.'
First performance: Worcester, Cathedral Church of Christ and St. Mary, 8
September 1896
Anna Williams (sop.), Jessie King (cont.), Edward Lloyd (ten.),
Watkin Mills (bass) with the Festival Chorus and Orchestra, conducted
by Edward Elgar
Novello, 1896

Scenes from the Saga of King Olaf (Op.30)
Cantata for STB soli, mixed chorus and orchestra
2.2+1.2+1.2/4.3.3.1/timp./perc./harp/organ/strings
Text: H.W. Longfellow and H.A. Acworth
Commissioned by Charles Swinnerton Heap for the 1896 North
Staffordshire Festival
'Charles Swinnerton Heap'
First performance: Hanley, 30 October 1896.
Medora Henson (sop.), Edward Lloyd (ten.), David Ffrangcon-Davies
(bass) with the Festival Chorus and Orchestra, conducted by Edward Elgar
First London: Crystal Palace, 3 April 1897
Soloists, Chorus and Orchestra, conducted by August Manns
Novello, 1896

1897

The Banner of St. George (Op.33)
Ballad for mixed chorus and orchestra
2+1.2.2.2/4.2 cor.2+1.1/timp./perc./organ/strings
Text: Shapcott Wensley
Commissioned by Novello & Co. Ltd.
First performance: London, Kensington, 18 May 1897
St. Cuthbert's Hall Choral Society and Orchestra, conducted by
Cyril Miller
Novello, 1897

Chanson de Nuit (Op.15 no.1)
for violin and piano or small orchestra
Originally composed with the title *Evensong*
1.1.2.1/2.0.0.0/harp/strings
'Dr. F. Ehrke' [violinist in the Worcester Philharmonic Orchestra]
First performance (orchestral version): London, Queen's Hall, 14
September 1901
Queen's Hall Orchestra, conducted by Henry Wood
Novello (violin and piano) 1897
Novello (orchestral) 1901

Grete Malverne on a rocke
Part song for mixed chorus
Text: 'Traditional'
Privately printed Christmas card, 1897
Published in 1909 by Novello as the carol *Lo! Christ the Lord is born* for
mixed chorus, text by Shapcott Wensley

Imperial March (Op.32)
for orchestra
Commissioned by Novello & Co. Ltd.
2+1.2.2.2+1/4.3.3.1/timp./perc./strings
First performance: London, Crystal Palace, 19 April 1897.
Crystal Palace Orchestra, conducted by August Manns
Novello, 1897

Love Alone will Stay (Lute Song)
Song for voice and piano
Text: C.A. Elgar (1848–1920)
The Dome, 1898
Incorporated into *Sea Pictures* (1899)

Minuet (Op.21)
for solo piano or small orchestra
1.1.2.1/2.0.0.0/timp./strings
'Paul Kilburn'
First performance (orch. version): New Brighton, 16 July 1899

New Brighton Tower Orchestra, conducted by Edward Elgar
The Dome, 1897
J. Williams, 1897 (piano) and 1899 (orchestral)

The Moods of Dan Illustrated
for solo piano
I.   He sleeps
II. He capers
Incomplete

Roundel
song for voice and piano
Text: A.C. Swinburne (1837–1909)
First performance: Worcester, Musical Union, 26 April 1897
Gertrude Walker and Edward Elgar (piano)

Te Deum and Benedictus (Op.34)
for mixed chorus and orchestra
2+1.0.2+1.2/4.3.3.1/timp./perc./organ/strings
Text: The Book of Common Prayer
Commissioned by G.R. Sinclair for the 1897 Three Choirs Festival
'G.R. Sinclair'
First performance: Hereford, Cathedral Church of Our Lady and St.
Ethelbert, 12 September 1897
Festival Chorus and Orchestra, conducted by G.R. Sinclair
Novello, 1897

1898

Caractacus (Op.35)
Cantata for soprano, tenor, baritone and bass soloists, mixed chorus and
orchestra
Text: H.A. Acworth
Commissioned by the 1898 Leeds Music Festival
2+1.2.2+1.2+1/4.4.3.1/timp./perc./organ/harp/strings
'Her most Gracious Majesty Queen Victoria'
First performance: Leeds, Town Hall, 5 October 1898
Medora Henson (sop.), Edward Lloyd (ten.), John Browning (bar.) and

Andrew Black (bass) with the Leeds Festival Chorus and Orchestra, conducted by Edward Elgar
First London: Royal Albert Hall, 20 April 1899
Medora Henson (sop.), Edward Lloyd (ten.), Douglas Powell (bar.) and Andrew Black (bass) with the Royal Choral Society and Orchestra, conducted by Edward Elgar
Novello, 1898

The Holly and the Ivy
Carol arranged for semi-chorus, mixed chorus and orchestra
2.2.2.2/2.2.2.1/timp./organ/harp/strings
First performance: Worcester, 7 January 1899
The Worcestershire Philharmonic Society and Chorus, conducted by Edward Elgar

The Moods of Dan Illustrated Nos. III–V
III. He muses (on the muzzling order)
IV. Dan uneasy
V. Dan Triumphant

1899

Chanson de Matin (Op.15 no.2)
for violin and piano or small orchestra
1.1.2.1/2.0.0.0/harp/strings
First performance (orchestral version): London, Queen's Hall, 14 September 1901.
Queen's Hall Orchestra, conducted by Henry Wood
Novello (violin and piano), 1899
Novello (orchestral), 1901

Dry those Fair, those Crystal Eyes
Song for voice and piano
Text: Henry King (1592–1669)
First performance: London, Royal Albert Hall, 21 June 1899.
Souvenir of the Charing Cross Hospital Bazaar, 1899

The Pipes of Pan
Song for voice and piano or orchestra
Text: A. Ross
2.2.2.2/4.2.1.0/timp./perc./harp/strings
First performance (voice and piano): London, Crystal Palace, 30 April 1900
Lilian Blouvelt
First performance (voice and orchestra): Bristol, Colston Hall, 10 October 1902.
Andrew Black (bass) and Orchestra, conducted by Edward Elgar
Boosey, 1900

Sea Pictures (Op.37)
Song cycle for contralto or mezzo-soprano and orchestra
1. Sea Slumber-Song
2. In haven (Capri)
3. Sabbath Morning at Sea
4. Where Corals Lie
5. The Swimmer
Texts: 1. Roden B.W. Noel (1834–1909)
      2. C.A. Elgar (1848–1920)
      3. E.B.Browning (1806–1861)
      4. Richard Garnett (1835–1906)
      5. Adam Lindsay Gordon (1833–1870)
2.2.2.2+1/4.2.3.1/timp./perc./organ/harp/strings
First performance: Norwich, St. Andrew's Hall, 5 October 1900
Clara Butt (contralto) and Festival Orchestra, conducted by Edward Elgar
Boosey, 1900

Sérénade Lyrique
Melodie for small orchestra
2.2.2.2/2.0.0.0/timp./harp/strings
Composed for Ivan Caryll's Orchestra
First performance: London, St. James's Hall, 27 November 1900
Ivan Caryll's orchestra
Chappell, 1899

Three Characteristic Pieces (Op.10)
for orchestra

1. Mazurka
2. Serenade Mauresque
3. Contrasts : The Gavotte A.D.1700 and 1900
2+1.2.2.2/4.2.3.1/timp./perc./strings
'Lady Mary Lygon'
First performance (as Opus 10): New Brighton, 16 July 1899
New Brighton Tower Orchestra, conducted by Edward Elgar
Novello, 1899

To her, beneath whose steadfast star
Part-song for mixed chorus and one of a collection dedicated to H.M.
Queen Victoria on the occasion of her 80th birthday
Text: Frederic W.H. Myers
First performance: Windsor, the Castle, 24 May 1899
Chorus conducted by Edward Elgar
Macmillan, 1899 (Choral Songs in Honour of H.M. Queen Victoria)

Variations on an Original Theme ('Enigma') (Op.36)
for orchestra
Theme (Enigma) (Andante)
Var. 1 C.A.E. (Andante)
Var. 2 H.D.S.-P. (Allegro)
Var. 3 R.B.T. (Allegretto)
Var. 4 W.M.B. (Allegro di molto)
Var. 5 R.P.A. (Moderato)
Var. 6 Ysobel (Andantino)
Var. 7 Troyte (Presto)
Var. 8 W.N. (Allegretto)
Var. 9 Nimrod (Adagio)
Var. 10 Intermezzo : Dorabella (Allegretto)
Var. 11 G.R.S. (Allegro di molto)
Var. 12 B.G.N. (Andante)
Var. 13 Romanza (* * *) (Moderato)
Var. 14 Finale, E.D.U. (Allegro)
2+1.2.2.2+1/4.3.3.1/timp./perc./organ/strings
'To my friends pictured within'
First performance: London, St. James's Hall, 19 June 1899
Orchestra conducted by Hans Richter

First performance with extended finale: Worcester, Public Hall, 13
September 1899
Orchestra conducted by Edward Elgar
Novello, 1899

1900

The Dream of Gerontius (Op.38)
for mezzo-soprano, tenor and bass soli, semi-chorus, mixed chorus and
orchestra
Text: Cardinal John Henry Newman (1801–1890)
Commissioned by the 1900 Birmingham Music Festival
2+1.2+1.2+1.2+1/4.3(+3 ad.lib.)3.1/timp./perc./organ/harp/strings
'A.D.G.M.' [Ad Majorem Dei Gloriam]
First performance: Birmingham, Town Hall, 3 October 1900
Marie Brema (mez.sop.), Edward Lloyd (ten.) and H.Plunkett Greene
(bass) with the Festival Chorus and Orchestra, conducted by Hans
Richter
First London: Westminster Cathedral, 6 June 1903
Muriel Foster (mez.sop.), Ludwig Wüllner (ten.) and David Ffrangcon-
Davies (bass) with the North Staffordshire Festival Chorus and Orchestra,
conducted by Edward Elgar
Novello, 1900

1901

Always and Everywhere
Song for voice and piano
Text: Count N.A.Z. Krasinsky, trans. from Polish by F.H. Fortey
First performance: unable to trace
Boosey, 1901

Cockaigne (In London Town) (Op.40)
Concert overture for orchestra
2+1.2.2.2+1/4.2.2 corn.3.1/timp./perc./organ/strings
'To my many friends the members of British orchestras'
First performance: London, Queen's Hall, 20 June 1901
Philharmonic Society Orchestra, conducted by Edward Elgar
Boosey, 1901

Come, gentle night
Song for voice and piano
Text: Clifton Bingham
First performance: London, Royal Albert Hall, 31 October 1901
Boosey, 1901

Concert Allegro
for solo piano
'For Fanny Davies'
First performance: London, St James's Hall, 2 December 1901.
Fanny Davies (piano)
Novello, 1973

Incidental Music for 'Grania and Diarmid' (Op.42)
for orchestra
Written for the Irish Literary Society's production
1. Incidental music
2. Funeral March
3. Song: 'There are seven that pull the thread'
Text: play by George Moore, song by W.B. Yeats
2.2+1.2+1.2+1/4.2.3.1/timp./perc./harp/strings
'Henry J.Wood'
First performance: Dublin, Gaiety Theatre, 21 October 1901.
First performance of *Funeral March* in London: Queen's Hall, 18 January 1902.
Queen's Hall Orchestra, conducted by Henry Wood
Novello, 1902

May Song
for solo piano, violin and piano, or small orchestra
1.1.2.1/2.2 corn.1.0/timp./perc./strings
'Inscribed to Mrs T. Garmston Hyde'
May Song was due to be performed by the Worcestershire Philharmonic Society Orchestra on 10 May 1902 but omitted as the concert was too long.
W.H.Broome, 1901
Elkin, 1928 (full score)

Orchestration of 'Emmaus' by A. Herbert Brewer
Cantata for soprano and tenor soli, mixed chorus and orchestra
2.2.2.2/2.2.3.1/timp./organ/harp/strings
First performance: Gloucester, Cathedral Church of the Holy Trinity, 12
September 1901
Emma Albani (sop.), Ben Davies (ten.) with the Three Choirs Festival
Chorus and Gloucester Festival Orchestra, conducted by A. Herbert
Brewer
Novello, 1901 (vocal score)

Pomp and Circumstance Military March in D major (Op.39 no.1)
for orchestra
2+1.2.2+1.2+1/4.2.2 corn.3.1/timp./perc./2 harps/organ/strings
'A.E.Rodewald and members of the Liverpool Orchestral Society'
First performance: Liverpool, 19 October 1901
The Liverpool Orchestral Society Orchestra, conducted by A.E. Rodewald
First London: Queen's Hall, 22 October 1901
Queen's Hall Orchestra, conducted by Henry Wood
Boosey, 1902

Pomp and Circumstance Military March in A minor (Op.39 no.2)
for orchestra
2+1.2.2+1.2+1/4.2.2 corn.3.1/timp./perc./strings
'Granville Bantock'
First performance: Liverpool, 19 October 1901
The Liverpool Orchestral Society Orchestra, conducted by A.E.Rodewald
First London: Queen's Hall, 22 October 1901
Queen's Hall Orchestra, conducted by Henry Wood
Boosey, 1902

Skizze
for solo piano
'Professor Julius Buths, Dusseldorf'
First performance: Shenley (Herts.), Ridgehurst, 17 January 1903
Edward Elgar (piano)
Musik-Beilag zur Neue Musik-Zeitung, XXIV (1903)
Novello, 1976

Viola parts for Mozart's Epistle Sonatas in C (K.328 and 336)
Originally scored for strings (without violas) and organ
First performance: Worcester, Public Hall, 17 January 1901
Worcestershire Philharmonic Society Orchestra and G.S.Chignell
(organ), conducted by Edward Elgar

'Welsh Overture'
for orchestra (fragment)

1902

Coronation Ode (Op.44)
for soprano, contralto, tenor and bass soli, mixed chorus (44 sopranos, 34
contraltos, 42 tenors and 40 basses), organ and orchestra
1. Crown the King with Life
2. Daughters of Ancient Kings
3. Britain, ask of thyself
4. Hark, upon the hallow'd air
5. Only let the heart be pure
6. Peace, gentle peace
7. Finale: Land of Hope and Glory
Text: A.C.Benson (1862–1925)
2+1.2.2+1.2+1/4.2.3.1/timp./perc./organ/harp/strings with
additional 36-piece military band
'H.M.King Edward VII (by special permission)'
First performance: Sheffield, 2 October 1902
Agnes Nicholls (sop.), Muriel Foster (mez.sop.), John Coates (ten.) and
David Ffrangcon-Davies (bass) with the Sheffield Festival Chorus and
Orchestra, conducted by Edward Elgar
First London: Queen's Hall, 26 October 1902
Soloists, Chorus and Orchestra, conducted by Edward Elgar
Boosey, 1902

Enfants d'un Rêve (Dream Children) (Op.43)
Two pieces for small orchestra after Charles Lamb
2.2.2.2/4.0.0.0/timp./harp/strings
First performance: London, Queen's Hall, 4 September 1902
Queen's Hall Orchestra, conducted by Arthur W. Payne

Williams, 1902 (piano score)
Schott, 1913 (full score)

From the Greek Anthology (Op.45)
Five part-songs for unaccompanied mens' voices (TTBB)
1. Yea, cast me from the heights of the mountain
2. Whether I find thee
3. After many a dusty mile
4. It's oh! to be a wild wind
5. Feasting I watch
Text: (1) Anon. (tr. Alma Strettell)
(2) Anon. (tr. Andrew Lang)
(3) Anon. (tr. Edmund Gosse)
(4) Anon. (tr. W.M. Hardinge)
(5) Marcus Argentarius (tr. Richard Garnett)
'Sir Walter Parratt'
First performance: London, Royal Albert Hall, 25 April 1904
Royal Choral Society, conducted by Arthur Fagge
Novello, 1903

God Save the King
Arranged for soprano solo, mixed chorus and orchestra
2+1.2.2.2+1/4.2.2 corn.3.1/timp./perc./organ/strings
First performance: unable to trace
Novello, 1902

In the Dawn (Op.41 no.1)
Song for voice and piano
Text: A.C.Benson (1862–1925)
First performance: unable to trace
Boosey, 1902

Land of Hope and Glory
Song for voice and piano
Arranged from *Pomp and Circumstance March No.1* (Op.39) and the
Coronation Ode (Op.44) with different words by A.C. Benson
First performance: London, Royal Albert Hall, 21 June 1902
Clara Butt (contralto)
Boosey, 1902

O Mightiest of the Mighty
Hymn for mixed chorus and organ
Text: Rev. S. Childs Clarke
'H.R.H. The Prince of Wales'
First performance: London, Westminster Abbey, 9 August 1902.
Coronation Choir, conducted by Frederick Bridge
(The Coronation of H.M. King Edward VII)
Novello, 1902

The Moods of Dan Illustrated No.VI
VI. Dan wistful

Speak Music (Op.41 no.2)
Song for voice and piano
Text: A.C. Benson (1862–1925)
'Mrs E. Speyer'
First performance: unable to trace
Boosey, 1902

Weary Wind of the West
Part-song for mixed chorus
Text: T.E. Brown (1830–1897)
'Composed for Morecambe Musical Festival'
First performance: Morecambe, 2 May 1903.
Novello, 1903

1903

The Apostles (Op.49)
Oratorio for soprano, contralto, tenor and three bass soloists, mixed
chorus and orchestra
Text: compiled by Elgar from *The Holy Bible* and other sources
Commissioned by the 1903 Birmingham Music Festival
2+1.2+1.2+1.2+1/4.3.3.1/timp./perc./organ/2 harps/strings
'A.D.G.M.'
First performance: Birmingham, Town Hall, 14 October 1903.
Emma Albani (sop.), Muriel Foster (cont.), John Coates (ten.), Robert
Kennerley-Rumford (bass), Andrew Black (bass) and David Ffrangcon-
Davies (bass) with the Birmingham Festival Chorus and Orchestra,
conducted by Edward Elgar

First London: Royal Opera House, Covent Garden, 15 March 1904
Agnes Nicholls (sop.), Louise Kirkby-Lunn (cont.), John Coates (ten.),
Robert Kennerley-Rumford (bass), Andrew Black (bass) and David
Ffrangcon-Davies (bass) with the Hallé Choir and Orchestra, conducted
by Hans Richter
Novello, 1903

Cockaigne No.2 ('City of Dreadful Night')
Concert overture for orchestra (fragment)

Fantasia for Strings
'Hans' [Richter]
Incomplete

The Moods of Dan Illustrated No. VII (New Series)
Retrospective. The Sinful Youth of Dan

Rabelais (Gargantua and Pantagruel)
Ballet (fragment)

Speak my Heart!
Song for voice and piano
Text: A.C. Benson (1862-1925)
Boosey, 1903

1904

Cadenza for C.H. Lloyd's 'Concerto for Organ and Orchestra'
First performance: Three Choirs Festival (Gloucester), September 1895
Elgar's cadenza was composed for the second performance:
Gloucester, Cathedral Church of the Holy Trinity, 7 September 1904.
G.R. Sinclair (organ) and the Festival Orchestra, conducted by C.H. Lloyd

In the South (Alassio) (Op.50)
Concert overture for orchestra
3+1.2+1.2+1.2+1/4.3.3.1/timp./perc./2 harps/strings
'To my friend Leo F. Schuster'
First performance: London, Royal Opera House, Covent Garden, 16

March 1904 (The Elgar Festival).
The Hallé Orchestra, conducted by Edward Elgar
Novello, 1904
Extract: *In Moonlight (Canto Popolare)*
for small orchestra; violin and piano; viola and piano; cello and piano;
clarinet and piano; organ;and as a song for high or medium voice and
piano
Text: P.B. Shelley (1792–1822)
First performance (with small orchestra): Hereford, 22 November 1902
Herefordshire Philharmonic Society Orchestra, conducted by G.R.
Sinclair

Pomp and Circumstance Military March in C minor (Op.39 no.3)
for orchestra
2+1.2+1.2+1.3+1/4.2.2 corn.3.1/timp./perc./strings
'Ivor Atkins'
First performance: London, Queen's Hall, 8 March 1905
The London Symphony Orchestra, conducted by Edward Elgar
Boosey, 1905

1905

April
Part-song for two sopranos, 2 violins and piano
Text: W.Watson (1858–1935)
Incomplete

Evening Song
Part-song for mixed voices
Text: Coventry Patmore (1823–1896)
'In memoriam R.G.H. Howson'
First performance: Morecambe, 12 May 1906.
Novello, 1906

In Smyrna
for solo piano
The Daily Mail, 'The Queen's Christmas Carol Book', 1905
Novello, 1976

Introduction and Allegro for String Quartet and String Orchestra
(Op.47)
'Professor S.S.Sanford, Yale University, U.S.A.'
First performance: London, Queen's Hall, 8 March 1905
The London Symphony Orchestra, with solo quartet: A.W. Payne, W.H. Eaynes, A. Hobbday and B.P. Parker, conducted by Edward Elgar
Novello, 1905

Ozymandias I
Scena for bass voice
Text: P.B. Shelley (1792–1822)
Incomplete

Scene: Callicles
Song for solo voice (for Muriel Foster)
Text: M. Arnold (1822–1888)
Incomplete

1906

For Dot's Nuns
for organ
'Helen Agnes Elgar'

The Kingdom (Op.51)
Oratorio for soprano, contralto, tenor and bass soloists, mixed chorus and orchestra
Text: compiled by Elgar from *The Holy Bible* and other sources
Commissioned by the 1906 Birmingham Music Festival
3+1.2+1.2+1.2+1/4.3.3.1/timp./perc./organ/2 harps/strings
'A.M.D.G.'
First performance: Birmingham Town Hall, 3 October 1906
Agnes Nicholls (sop.), Muriel Foster (cont.), John Coates (ten.) and William Higley (bass) with Festival Chorus and Orchestra, conducted by Edward Elgar
First London: Alexandra Palace, 17 November 1906
Cicely Gleeson-White (sop.), Edna Thornton (cont.), John Coates (ten.) and Dalton Baker (bass) with the Alexandra Palace Chorus and Orchestra, conducted by Allen Gill
Novello, 1906

The Last Judgement
Oratorio, completing the third part of the trilogy
Incomplete

1907

Andantino
for violin, mandoline and guitar
Unfinished

A Christmas Greeting (Op.52)
Carol for two sopranos, male chorus(TB) ad.lib., 2 violins and piano
Text: C.A. Elgar (1848–1920)
'Dr. G.R. Sinclair and the choristers of Hereford Cathedral'
First performance: Hereford, Town Hall, 1 January 1908
Choristers of Hereford Cathedral, conducted by G.R. Sinclair
Novello, 1908

Follow the Colours: Marching Song for Soldiers
Song for unison voices and orchestra
Text: Capt. de Courcy Stretton
'William de Courcy Stretton'
First performance: London, Royal Albert Hall, 24 May 1908
Novello, 1908

Four Part-Songs (Op.53)
for mixed voices
1.   There is sweet music
2.   Deep in my soul
3.   O Wild West Wind
4.   Owls (An Epitaph)
Text: (1) Alfred, Lord Tennyson (1809–1892)
(2) Lord Byron (1788–1824)
(3) P.B. Shelley (1792–1822)
(4) E.W. Elgar (1857–1934)
(1) 'Canon Gorton' (2) 'Julia H. Worthington' (3) 'W.G. McNaught' (4)
'Pietro d'Alba' [Peter Rabbit]
Novello, 1908

How Calmly the Evening
Part-song for mixed voices
Text: T.T. Lynch
Novello, 1908

Love (Op.18 no.2)
Part-song for mixed voices
Text: Arthur Maquarie
'Caroline Alice Elgar'
Novello, 1907

Pomp and Circumstance Military March in G (Op.39 no.4)
for orchestra
2+1.2+1.2+1.2+1/4.3.3.1/timp./perc./harp/strings
'G.R. Sinclair'
First performance: London, Queen's Hall, 24 August 1907
Queen's Hall Orchestra, conducted by Edward Elgar
Boosey, 1907

Quartet for Strings
for 2 violins, viola and cello (fragment)

The Reveille (Op.54)
Part-song for male voices (TTBB)
Text: F.Bret Harte (1836–1902)
'Henry C.Embleton'
First performance: Blackpool, 17 October 1908
Novello, 1908

Six Chants
for mixed voices
Text: Book of the Psalms
Novello, 1909

The Wand of Youth Suite No.1 (Op.1a)
for orchestra
1. Overture
2. Serenade

3. Minuet
4. Sun Dance
5. Fairy Pipers
6. Slumber Scene
7. Fairies and Giants

2+1.2.2.2+1/4.2.3.1/timp./perc./harp/strings
'C. Lee Williams'
First performance: London, Queen's Hall, 14 December 1907
Queen's Hall Orchestra, conducted by Henry Wood
Novello, 1907

1908

In Memoriam: Silence and Sorrow
Incomplete song, dated 2 June 1908
'In memory of a seer '
Michael Kennedy says that this may have been a work planned to
commemorate Jaeger, whose death was by then inevitable.

Orchestration of the Coda of J.S. Bach's Toccata in F (S.540)
3.2+1.2+1.2+1/4.3.3.1/timp./perc./organ/strings
First performance: Worcester, Cathedral Church of Christ and St.Mary, 6
September 1908

Pleading (Op.48 no.1)
Song for voice and piano or small orchestra
1.0.2.2/corn.2.0.0/piano/harp/strings
Text: A.L. Salmon
'Lady Maud Warrender'
First performance: Hereford, November 1908
Lady Maud Warrender and Edward Elgar (piano)
Novello, 1908

Symphony No.1 in Ab (Op.55)
for orchestra
1. Andante, Nobilmente e semplice - Allegro
2. Allegro Molto
3. Adagio

4. Lento–Allegro
3+1.2+1.2+1.2+1/4.3.3.1/timp./perc./2 harps/strings
'Hans Richter, Mus.Doc.True artist and true friend'
First performance: Manchester, Free Trade Hall, 3 December 1908
The Halle Orchestra, conducted by Hans Richter
First London: Queen's Hall, 7 December 1908
The London Symphony Orchestra, conducted by Hans Richter
Novello, 1908

The Wand of Youth Suite No. 2 (Op.1b)
for orchestra
1. March
2. The Little Bells
3. Moths and Butterflies
4. Fountain Dance
5. The Tame Bear
6. The Wild Bears
2+1.2.2.2+1/4.2.3.1/timp./perc./strings
'Hubert A.Leicester'
First performance: Worcester, Public Hall, 9 September 1908
Orchestra conducted by Edward Elgar
First London: Queen's Hall, 17 October 1908
Queen's Hall Orchestra, conducted by Edward Elgar
Novello, 1908

1909

Angelus (Tuscany) (Op.56 no.1)
Part song for mixed voices
Text: Traditional Tuscan, adapted by Elgar
'Mrs Charles Stuart Wortley'
First performance: Royal Albert Hall, 8 December 1910
Novello, 1909

A Child Asleep
Song for voice and piano
Text: E.B. Browning (1806–1861)
'Anthony Goetz [Muriel Foster's son], for his mother's singing'
Novello, 1910

Elegy (Op.58)
for string orchestra
'In memoriam late Junior Warden of Worshipful Company of Musicians,
Rev. R.H. Hadden, M.A.'
First performance: London, the Mansion House, 13 July 1909
Novello, 1910

Go Song of Mine (Op.57)
Part-song for double mixed voices
Text: G.Cavalcanti, trans. D.G.Rossetti
'Alfred H.Littleton'
First performance: Hereford, 9 September 1909
Chorus conducted by G.R. Sinclair
Novello, 1909

In a Vineyard
Choral Suite
1.   Introduction
2.   In a Vineyard
3.   Angelus
4.   Dance
5.   Vintage
6.   Envoi
Text (some): W.S. Landon
Incomplete

Opera in Three Acts
Thematic fragments

Scherzo for Piano and Orchestra
Fragment

Song Cycle (Op.59 nos.1–6)
for mezzo soprano and piano or orchestra
1.   Proem (Incomplete)
2.   The Waking (Incomplete)
3.   Oh, soft was the Song
4.   There is an Orchard (Incomplete)
5.   Was it some Golden Star?
6.   Twilight

Text: Gilbert Parker (1862–1932)
2.2.2.2/2.0.0.0/timp./harp/strings
First performance: London, Queen's Hall, 24 January 1910.
Muriel Foster (m.s.) and Queen's Hall Orchestra, conducted by Edward
Elgar (the Jaeger Memorial Concert)
Novello, 1910

They are at rest
Anthem for unaccompanied mixed voices
Text: Cardinal John Henry Newman
First performance: Windsor, Royal Mausoleum, 22 January 1910
Novello, 1901

Tuscan Fantastico in Ab
Fragment

Two Songs (Op.60)
for voice and piano or orchestra
1. The Torch
2. The River
2+1.2+1.2+1.2+1/4.3.3.1/timp./perc./harp/strings
Texts: E. Elgar: folk songs from Easter Europe 'paraphrased by P[ietro]
d'Alba [pseud.] and E. Elgar.' Two further numbers were planned: *The
Shrine* and *The Bee*.
'Yvonne'
First performance: Hereford, 11 September 1912
Muriel Foster (m.s.) and orchestra, conducted by G.R. Sinclair
Novello, 1910

1910

Concerto for Violin and Orchestra in B minor (Op.61)
1. Allegro
2. Andante
3. Allegro molto
2.2.2.2+1/4.2.3.1/timp./strings
'Fritz Kreisler'
On the score is inscribed a quotation in Spanish: 'Aqui esta encerrada el

alma de..... (1910)' ['Here is enshrined the soul of.....']
First performance: London, Queen's Hall, 10 November 1910
Fritz Kreisler (violin) and the Philharmonic Society Orchestra, conducted
by Edward Elgar
Novello, 1910

The King's Way
Song for voice and piano
Text: C.A. Elgar (1848–1920)
First performance: London, Alexandra Palace, 15 January 1910.
Clara Butt (contralto)
Boosey, 1910

Romance for Bassoon and Orchestra (Op.62)
2.2.2.2/3.0.3.0/timp./strings
'Edwin F.James'
First performance: Hereford, 16 February 1911
Edwin F. James (bassoon) and Orchestra, conducted by Edward Elgar
Novello, 1910

1911

Arrangements of Two Chorales from J.S. Bach's St. Matthew Passion
1.   O Mensch bewein dein Sünde gross
2.   O Haupt voll Blut und Wunden
4 horns, 3trumpets, 3 trombones and tuba
First performance: Worcester, tower of the Cathedral Church of Christ and
St. Mary, 14 September 1911

Coronation March (Op.65)
for orchestra
2+1.2+1.2+1.2+1/4.3.3.1/timp./perc./organ/2 harps/strings
First performance: London, Westminster Abbey, 22 June 1911
Coronation Orchestra, conducted by Frederick Bridge
Novello, 1912

Edition of J.S. Bach's St. Matthew Passion
Prepared with Ivor Atkins

First performance: Worcester, Cathedral Church of Christ and St. Mary, 14 September 1911
Soloists included Agnes Nicholls, Louise Kirkby Lunn and Gervase Elwes with Fritz Kreisler (violin), the Three Choirs Festival Chorus and Worcester Festival Orchestra, conducted by Ivor Atkins

O Hearken Thou (Intende voci orationis meae) (Op.64)
Offertory for mixed chorus and orchestra
Text: Psalm V v.1 for *Offertorium*, Psalm V vv.2–3 for Anthem
2.0.2.2/2.0.0.0/timp./organ/strings
First performance: London, Westminster Abbey, 22 June 1911
Coronation Choir and Orchestra, conducted by Frederick Bridge
Novello, 1911

Symphony No.2 in Eb major (Op.63)
for orchestra
1.   Allegro vivace e nobilmente
2.   Larghetto
3.   Rondo : Presto
4.   Moderato e maestoso
2+1.2+1.2+1.2+1/4.3.3.1/timp./perc./2 harps/strings
'to the memory of His Late Majesty King Edward VII'
First performance: London, Queen's Hall, 24 May 1911
Queen's Hall Orchestra, conducted by Edward Elgar
Novello, 1911

1912

The Crown of India (Op.66)
for contralto and bass soloists, mixed chorus and orchestra
Tableau 1. The Cities of Ind
1a.   Introduction
1b.   Sacred Measures
2.   Dance of Nautch Girls
2a.   India greets her cities
3.   Hail, Immemorial Ind!
3a.   Entrance of Calcutta
3b.   Entrance of Delhi
4a.   Introduction

4b. March of Mogul Emperors
5. Entrance of 'John Company'
5a. Entrance of St.George
6. Rule of England
7. Interlude

Tableau II. Ave Imperator!
8a. Introduction
8b. Warrior's Dance
9. Cities of India
10. March. The Crown of India
10a. The Homage of Ind
11. Crowning of Delhi
12. Ave Imperator!
Text: Henry Hamilton
2+1.2+1.2+1.2+1/4.3.3.1/timp./perc./harp/strings
First performance: London, Coliseum Theatre, 11 March 1912
Marion Bealy (cont.) and Harry Dearth (bass) and Orchestra, conducted by Edward Elgar
Enoch, 1912

The Crown of India (Op.66)
Suite for orchestra
1. Introduction Dance of Nautch Girls
2. Menuetto
3. Warrior's dance
4. Intermezzo
5. March of the Mogul Emperors
2+1.2+1.2+1.2+1/4.3.3.1/timp./perc./harp.strings
First performance: Hereford, Shire Hall, 11 September 1912
The London Symphony Orchestra, conducted by Edward Elgar
Hawkes, 1912

Great is the Lord (Op.67)
Anthem for double mixed chorus and organ or orchestra
Written for the Royal Society
Text: Psalm 48
2.2.2.2+1/4.2.3.1/timp./organ/strings

'Very Rev. J. Armitage Robinson, D.D., Dean of Wells'
First performance: London, Westminster Abbey, 16 July 1912.
Resident choir and organist, conducted by Frederick Bridge
Novello, 1912

The Music Makers (Op.69)
Ode for contralto or mezzo soprano, mixed chorus and orchestra
Text: Arthur W.E. O'Shaughnessy (1844–1881)
2+1.2+1.1.2+1/4.3.3.1/timp./perc./organ/2 harps/strings
'My friend Nicholas Kilburn'
First performance: Birmingham, Town Hall, 1 October 1912
Muriel Foster (cont.) with the Birmingham Festival Chorus and Orchestra,
conducted by Edward Elgar
First London: Royal Albert Hall, 28 November 1912
Muriel Foster (cont.) with the Royal Choral Society and Orchestra,
conducted by Frederick Bridge
Novello, 1912

1913

Carissima
for small orchestra
2.2.2.2/2.2 corn.0.0/timp./harp/strings
'Winifred Stephens' [Muriel Foster's sister]
First performance: London, Gramophone Company Studio, 21 January
1914.
Symphony Orchestra, conducted by Edward Elgar
First public performance: London, Royal Albert Hall, 15 February 1914
Royal Albert Orchestra, conducted by Landon Ronald
Elkin, 1914

Falstaff (Op.68)
Symphonic Study in C minor with two interludes for orchestra
Commissioned by the 1913 Leeds Music Festival
2+1.2+1.2.2+1/4.3.3.1/timp./perc./2 harps/strings
'Landon Ronald'
First performance: Leeds, Town Hall, 1 October 1913
The London Symphony Orchestra, conducted by Edward Elgar

First London: Queen's Hall, 3 November 1913
Queen's Hall Orchestra, conducted by Landon Ronald
Novello, 1913

1914

Arabian Serenade
Song for voice and piano
Text: Margery Lawrence
Boosey, 1914

The Birthright
Unison song for boys with bugles and drums
Text: G.A. Stocks
Novello, 1914

The Brook
Song for childrens' voices and piano
Text: Ellen Soule
Silver, Burdett & Co., New York, 1915

Carillon (Op.75)
Recitation for speaker and orchestra
Text: Emile Cammaerts (1878–1953)
2+1.2.2+1.2/4.2.3.1/timp.perc./organ/2 harps/strings
First performance: London, Queen's Hall, 7 December 1914
Tita Brand Cammaerts (rec.) and Queen's Hall Orchestra, conducted
by Edward Elgar
Elkin, 1914

The Chariots of the Lord
Song for voice and piano
Text: John Brownlie
First performance: London, Royal Albert Hall, 28 June 1914
Boosey, 1914

Death on the Hills (Op.72)
Choral-song for mixed voices
Text: A.N. Maikov, trans. Rosa Newmarch

'Lady Colvin'
Novello, 1914

Fear not O Lord
Harvest anthem of mixed chorus and organ
Text: Book of Joel, Ch.II, vv.21–4
Novello, 1914

Give Unto the Lord (Op.74)
Anthem for bass soloist, mixed chorus and organ or orchestra
Written for the 1914 Sons of the Clergy Festival
Text: Psalm 29
2.2.2.2/4.2.3.1/timp./perc./organ/strings
'Sir George Martin, M.V.O., Mus.D.'
First performance: London, St.Paul's Cathedral, 30 April 1914
Novello, 1914

The Merry-go-round
Song for childrens' voices and piano
Text: Florence C. Cox
Silver, Burdett & Co., New York, 1915

Soldier's Song: The Roll Call
A War Song for voice and piano, or orchestra (?)
Text: Harold Begbie
First performance: London, 10 October 1914
Clara Butt (contralto)

Sospiri (Op.70)
for strings, harp and organ
'W.H. Reed'
First performance: London, Queen's Hall, 15 August 1915
Queen's Hall Orchestra, conducted by Henry Wood
Breitkopf & Hartel, 1914

Two Choral Songs (Op.71)
for unaccompanied mixed chorus
1. The Shower
2. The Fountain

Text: Henry Vaughan (1622–1695)
1. 'Miss Frances Smart, Malvern'
2. 'W. Mann Dyson, Worcester'
Novello, 1914

Two Choral Songs (Op.73)
for unaccompanied mixed chorus
1. Love's Tempest
2. Serenade
Text: A.N. Maikov, trans. Rosa Newmarch
1. 'C. Sanford Terry'
2. 'Percy C. Hull'
Novello, 1914

The Windlass Song
Song for childrens' voices and piano
Text: W. Allingham (1824–1889)
Silver, Burdett & Co., New York, 1915

1915

Polonia (Op.76)
Symphonic prelude for orchestra
2+1.2.2+1.2+1/4.3.3.1/timp./perc./organ/2 harps/strings
'I.J. Paderewski'
First performance: London, Queen's Hall, 6 July 1915.
The London Symphony Orchestra, conducted by Edward Elgar. (A Polish
Victims' Relief Fund Concert)
Elkin, 1915

The Starlight Express (Op.78)
Incidental music for the play by Violet Pearn, based on the story *A Prisoner
in Fairyland* by Algernon Blackwood, and comprising orchestral entr'actes
and songs for soprano and baritone soloists:

Baritone Songs
'To the children'
'The Blue-eyes fairy'

'Curfew Song (Orion)'
'Night Winds'
'My old tunes'
'They're all soft-shining now'
Duet: 'Hearts must be soft-shiny dressed'

Soprano Songs
'I'm everywhere'
'Oh star, shine brightly'
'We shall meet the morning spiders'
'Dandelions, Daffodils'
'Laugh a little ev'ry day'
'Oh, think beauty'
Duet: 'Hearts must be soft-shiny dressed'

2.2.2.1/2.2.2.0/timp./percussion including cow bells, wind machine and barrel organ/harp/strings
First performance: London, Kingsway Theatre, 29 December 1915.
Clytie Hine (sop.) and Charles Mott (bar.) with Theatre
Orchestra, conducted by Julius Harrison
Elkin, 1916

Une Voix dans le Désert (Op.77)
Recitation with orchestra, including the song: 'Quand nos bourgeons se rouviront' for solo soprano
Text: Emile Cammaerts (1878–1953), trans. Tita Brand Cammaerts
2.0.2.2/4.2.3.0/timp./strings
First performance: London, Shaftsbury Theatre, 29 January 1916
Carlo Litten (reciter), Olga Lynn (sop.) and Orchestra,
conducted by Edward Elgar
Elkin, 1916

1916

Le Drapeau Belge (Op.79)
Recitation for speaker and orchestra
Text: Emile Cammaerts (1878–1953), trans.Lord Curzon
2+1.2+1.2+1.2+1/4.3.3.1/perc./strings
First performance: London, Queen's Hall, 14 April 1917.

Carlo Litten (rec.) and Queen's Hall Orchestra, conducted by Hamilton Harty
Elkin, 1916

Fight for Right
Song for mixed chorus and piano
Text: William Morris (1834–1896)
'Members of the Fight for Right Movement'
First performance: London, Queen's Hall, March 1916
Gervase Elwes (tenor)
Elkin, 1916

The Spirit of England (Op.80)
for soprano or tenor solo, mixed chorus and orchestra
1.   The Fourth of August
2.   To Women
3.   For the Fallen
Text: Laurence Binyon (1869–1943)
2+1.2+1.2+1.2+1/4.0.3.1/timp./perc./organ/2 harps/strings
'To the memory of our glorious men, with a special thought for the Worcesters'
First performances:
1. Birmingham, 4 October 1917
Rosina Buckman (sop.) and Orchestra, conducted by Appleby Matthews
2. Leeds, Town Hall, 3 May 1916.
John Booth (ten.), the Leeds Choral Union and
Orchestra, conducted by Edward Elgar
3. Leeds, Town Hall, 3 May 1916
Agnes Nicholls (sop.), the Leeds Choral Union and
Orchestra, conducted by Edward Elgar
First London (nos. 2 and 3): Queen's Hall, 8 May 1916
First complete performance: London, Royal Albert Hall, 24 November 1917
Agnes Nicholls (sop.) and Gervase Elwes (ten.), Chorus
and Orchestra, conducted by Edward Elgar
Novello, 1917

With Proud Thanksgiving
for mixed chorus and orchestra

Arranged in 1920 from *For the Fallen*, with accompaniment for
military or brass band (or for organ or piano) and used at the dedication of
the Cenotaph in Whitehall
It was orchestrated in April 1921 in response to a request for a work to
celebrate the Jubilee of the Royal Albert Hall and the Royal Choral Society
Text: Laurence Binyon (1869–1943)
2+1.2+1.2+1.2+1/4.3.3.1/timp./perc./organ/2 harps/strings
'The League of Arts'
First performance: London, Royal Albert Hall, 7 May 1921
The Royal Choral Society, the Royal Choral Society Orchestra and Royal
Albert Hall Orchestra, conducted by Edward Elgar
Novello, 1920

1917

The Fringes of the Fleet
Four songs for four baritones and orchestra
1. The Lowestoft Boat
2. Fate's Discourtesy
3. Submarines
4. The Sweepers
Text: Rudyard Kipling (1865–1936)
2.2.2.2/2.2.3.1/timp./perc. including sandpaper/strings
'Admiral Lord Beresford'
First performance: London, Coliseum Theatre, 11 June 1917
Charles Mott, Harry Barratt, Frederick Henry and Frederick Stewart with
the theatre orchestra, conducted by Edward Elgar
Enoch, 1917

Inside the Bar, A Sailor's Song
Song for four baritones and orchestra
Text: Gilbert Parker (1862–1932)
2.2.2.2/2.2.3.1/timp./perc./strings
'The 4 Singers'
First performance: Added to *Fringes of the Fleet* and first performed at the
London Coliseum, 25 June 1917, by the above singers
Enoch, 1917

Ozymandias II
Song for mezzo soprano and orchestra
Text: P.B. Shelley (1792–1822)
Incomplete

The Sanguine Fan (Op.81)
Music for Mrs Christopher Lowther's Ballet
2+1.1.2.2/4.2.3.0/timp./perc./harp/strings
First performance: London, Chelsea Palace Theatre, 20 March 1917
Theatre Orchestra, conducted by Elgar as part of the revue
'Chelsea on Tiptoe'
Elkin ('Echo's Dance'), 1917

1918

Big Steamers
Song for unison chorus and piano
Text: Rudyard Kipling (1865–1936)
Teacher's World (19 June 1918)

Quartet for Strings in E minor (Op.83)
1.   Allegro moderato
2.   Piacevole (poco andante)
3.   Allegro molto
'The Brodsky Quartet'
First performance (private):   Hampstead (London), Severn House, 7 January 1919
The British String Quartet: Albert Sammons, W.H. Reed (violins), Raymond Jeremy (viola) and Felix Salmond (cello)
First performance (public) : London, Wigmore Hall, 21 May 1919
The British String Quartet
Novello, 1919

Sonata for Violin and Piano in E minor (Op.82)
1.   Allegro
2.   Romance
3.   Allegro, non troppo
'Marie Joshua'

First performance (private): Hampstead (London), Severn House, 14 October 1918
W.H. Reed (violin) and Edward Elgar (piano)
First performance (public): London, Aeolian Hall, 21 March 1919
W.H. Reed (violin) and Landon Ronald (piano)
Novello, 1918

1919

Concerto for Violoncello and Orchestra in E minor (Op.85)
1. Adagio – Moderato
2. Lento – Allegro
3. Adagio
4. Allegro

2+1.2.2.2/4.2.3.1/timp./strings
'To Sidney and Frances Colvin'
First performance: London, Queen's Hall, 27 October 1919
Felix Salmond (cello) and the London Symphony Orchestra, conducted by Edward Elgar
Novello, 1919
Arranged as a *Viola Concerto* by Lionel Tertis
First performance: London, Queen's Hall, 21 March 1930
Lionel Tertis (viola) and the BBC Symphony Orchestra, conducted by Edward Elgar
Novello, 1929 (Arrangement for viola and piano by Lionel Tertis)

Quintet for Strings and Piano in A minor (Op.84)
1. Moderato
2. Adagio
3. Andante–Allegro

'Ernest Newman'
First performance (private): Hampstead (London), Severn House, 7 January 1919 (1st movement only)
The British String Quartet with William Murdoch (piano)
First complete performance (private): London, 26 April 1919
The British String Quartet with William Murdoch (piano)
First public performance: London, Wigmore Hall, 21 May 1919

The British String Quartet with William Murdoch (piano)
Novello, 1919

1921

Fugue in C minor: J.S. Bach, S.537 (Op.86)
Transcribed for orchestra
2+1.2+1.2+1.2+1/4.3.3.1/timp./perc./2 harps/strings
First performance: London, Queen's Hall, 27 October 1921
Goossens Orchestra, conducted by Eugene Goossens
Novello, 1921

1922

Fantasia in C minor: J.S. Bach, S.537 (Op.86)
Transcribed for orchestra
2+1.2+1.2+1.2+1/4.3.3.1/timp./perc./2 harps/strings
First performance: Gloucester, Cathedral Church of the Holy Trinity, 7
September 1922.
The London Symphony Orchestra, conducted by Edward Elgar
Novello, 1922

Jerusalem: C. Hubert H. Parry
Arranged for mixed chorus and orchestra
This arrangement was undertaken as a tribute to C.H.H. Parry's memory. It
was orchestrated for the opening concert of this Festival (and for this
occasion only)
2+1.2+1.2+1.2+1/4.3.3.1/timp./perc./organ/2 harps/strings
First performance: Leeds, Town Hall, 5 October 1922
Leeds Festival Chorus and the London Symphony Orchestra, conducted by
Hugh Allen

1923

Abide with me: Anthem by Ivor Atkins (written in 1907)
Arranged for mixed chorus and orchestra
2.2.2.2+1./4.3.3.1/timp./organ/harp/strings
First performance: Worcester, Cathedral Church of Christ and St. Mary,
2 September 1923

Festival Chorus and London Symphony Orchestra, conducted by Ivor Atkins
Unpublished

Arthur
Incidental music to Laurence Binyon's tragedy
2+1.0.1.0/2 corn. 0.1.0/timp./perc./piano/harp/strings
First performance: London, Old Vic, 12 March 1923
Theatre Orchestra, conducted by Edward Elgar (1st night only)
Chandos Music, 1973

Fugue in C minor
for solo piano
First performance: Worcester, Cathedral Church of Christ and St. Mary, 16 April 1925
Ivor Atkins (in an arrangement for organ)
Keith Prowse, 1932 (organ arrangement)

Let us lift up our Heart: Anthem by S.S. Wesley
Arranged for mixed soli, chorus and orchestra
First performance: Worcester, Cathedral Church of Christ and St. Mary, 6 September 1923
Dorothy Silk and Elsie Suddaby (sopranos), Astra Desmond (mezzo sop.), Steuart Wilson (ten.) and Norman Allin (bass) with the Three Choirs Festival Chorus and London Symphony Orchestra, conducted by Ivor Atkins
Unpublished

Memorial Chimes for a Carillon
Specially composed for the Opening of the Loughborough War Memorial Carillon
'Dr. W. Wooding Starmer'
First performance: Loughborough, 22 July 1923
Jef Denyn (carillon)
Unpublished
Elgar also arranged the work for organ

O Lord look down from Heaven: Anthem by J.Battishill
Arranged for mixed chorus and orchestra

First performance: Worcester, Cathedral Church of Christ and St.Mary, 6 September 1923
Three Choirs Festival Chorus and London Symphony Orchestra, conducted by Ivor Atkins
Unpublished

Overture in D minor: G.F. Handel (from *Chandos Anthem II*)
Transcribed for orchestra
2+1.2+1.2+1.2+1/4.3.3.1/timp./perc./organ/strings
First performance: Worcester, Cathedral Church of Christ and St. Mary, 2 September 1923
The London Symphony Orchestra, conducted by Edward Elgar
Novello, 1923

Two songs to words by John Drinkwater
for voice and piano
Text : John Drinkwater (1882–1937)
1.   Moonlit Apples
2.   Birthright
Incomplete

The Wanderer
Part-song for mens' voices (TTBB)
Text: Edward Elgar, adapted from *Wit and Drollery*, 1661
First performance: London, Wigmore Hall, 13 November 1923
The De Reszke Singers
Novello, 1923

Zut! Zut! Zut!
Part-song for mens' voices (TTBB)
Text: Edward Elgar, under the pseudonym of Richard Mardon
First performance: London, Wigmore Hall, 13 November 1923
The De Reszke Singers
Novello, 1923

1924

Empire March
for orchestra

Written for the opening ceremony of the British Empire Exhibition
in April 1924 but not played
2+1.2+1.2+1.2+1/4.3.3.1/timp./perc./organ/harp/strings
First performance: London, Wembley Stadium, 21 July 1924
Orchestra, conducted by Henry Jaxon
Boosey, 1924
Enoch, 1924 (piano solo)

Pageant of Empire
Eight songs for solo voice or mixed chorus and orchestra
1. Shakespeare's Kingdom
2. The Islands: A Song of New Zealand
3. The Blue Mountains : A Song of Australia
4. The Heart of Canada
5. Sailing Westward
6. Merchant Adventurers
7. The Immortal Legions
8. A Song of Union (chorus)
Text: Alfred Noyes (1880-1958)
2+1.2.2.2/4.3.2+1.1/timp./perc./harp/strings
First performance: London, Wembley Stadium, 21 July 1924.
Chorus and orchestra, conducted by Henry Jaxon
Enoch, 1924

1925

The Herald
Part-song for mens' voices (TTBB)
Text: Alexander Smith (1829–1867)
Novello, 1925

The Prince of Sleep
Part-song for mixed voices
Text: Walter De La Mare (1873–1956)
Elkin, 1925

1927

Civic Fanfare
for orchestra
Written for the Opening Service of the 1927 Three Choirs Festival, Hereford, and the mayoral procession
2+1.2+1.2+1.2+1/4.3.3.1/timp./perc./organ/strings (no violins)
First performance: Hereford, Cathedral Church of Our Lady and St. Ethelbert, 4 September 1927
The London Symphony Orchestra, conducted by Edward Elgar
Acuta Music, 1991

1928

Beau Brummel
Incidental music to Bertram P. Matthews play
Commissioned by Gerald Lawrence
2.2.2.2/2.2 corn.3.1/timp./perc./strings
First performance: Birmingham, Theatre Royal, 5 November 1928
Theatre Orchestra, conducted by Edward Elgar
Elkin (Minuet), 1929

I sing the birth
Carol for mixed voices
Text: Ben Jonson (1573–1637)
'Rev.Harcourt B.S.Fowler, Elmley Castle, Worcs.'
First performance: London, Royal Albert Hall, 10 December 1928.
Royal Choral Society, conducted by Malcolm Sargent
Novello, 1928

1929

Good Morrow
A simple carol [for mixed voices] for His Majesty's happy recovery
Text: G. Gascoigne (c.1534–1577)
First performance: Windsor, St. George's Chapel, 9 December 1929
St. George's Chapel choir, conducted by Walford Davies
Novello, 1929

I gave my heart unto my love
Song for voice and piano
Text: Edward Elgar (1857–1934)
Incomplete

It isnae me
Song for voice and piano
Text: Sally Holmes
'Joan Elwes'
First performance: Dumfries, October 1930.
Joan Elwes (soprano)
Keith Prowse, 1931

Jehova, quam multi sunt hostes mei: Motet by Henry Purcell
Arranged for mixed chorus and orchestra
2.2.2.2+1/4/2/3/1/timp./organ/strings
First performance: Worcester, Cathedral Church of Christ and St. Mary, 10 September 1929
Festival Chorus and London Symphony Orchestra, conducted by Ivor Atkins
Unpublished

1930

Nursery Suite
for orchestra
1. Aubade (Awake)
2. The Serious Doll
3. Busy-ness!
4. The Sad Doll
5. The Wagon Passes
6. The Merry Doll
7. Dreaming – Envoy
2+1.2.2.2/4.2.3.1/timp./perc./strings
'Their Royal Highnesses the Duchess of York, and the Princesses Elizabeth and Margaret Rose'
First performance (H.M.V. recording session): London, Kingsway Hall, 23 May 1931

The London Symphony Orchestra, conducted by Edward Elgar
First public performance: London, Queen's Hall, 20 August 1931
The London Symphony Orchestra, conducted by Edward Elgar
Keith Prowse, 1931

Pomp and Circumstance Military March in C major (Op.39 no.5)
for orchestra
2+1.2+1.2+1.2+1/4.3.3.1/timp./perc./strings
'Percy C. Hull'
First performance (H.M.V. recording session): London, Kingsway Hall, 18
September 1930.
The London Symphony Orchestra, conducted by Edward Elgar
First public performance: London, Queen's Hall, 20 September 1930
Queen's Hall Orchestra, conducted by Henry Wood
Boosey, 1930

Severn Suite (Op.87)
for brass band (scored by Henry Geehl) or orchestra
1. Introduction (Worcester Castle)
2. Toccata (Tournament)
3. Fugue (Cathedral)
4. Minuet (Commandery)
5. Coda
Sop.(Eb), solo corn.(Bb), ripeano (Bb), flugel(Bb), 2 corn.(Bb), solo hn.
(Eb), 2 hn. (Eb), 2 bar. (Bb), 2 trb. (Bb), b.trb., euph. (Bb), Eb bass, Bb
bass, drums
'G. Bernard Shaw'
First performance: London, Crystal Palace, 27 September 1930
Foden's Motor Works Band, conducted by Fred Mortimer
(The 1930 Brass Band National Championships Test-Piece)
R.Smith, 1930

Arranged for orchestra (1932)
2+1.2+1.2+1.2+1/4.3.3.1/timp./perc./strings
First performance: London, E.M.I. Abbey Road recording studio, 14 April
1932.
The London Symphony Orchestra, conducted by Edward Elgar
First public performance: Worcester, Cathedral Church of Christ and St.
Mary, 7 September 1932.

The London Symphony Orchestra, conducted by Edward Elgar
Keith Prowse [1932]
Acuta Music, 1991
Arranged for organ as *Organ Sonata No.2 in Bb* (Op.87a) by Ivor Atkins
Keith Prowse, 1933

1931

Suite for Oboe and Orchestra
Incomplete
'Leon Goossens'
First performance: one movement, *Soliloquy for oboe* (orchestrated by Gordon Jacob), performed on B.B.C. Television, 11 June 1967.
Leon Goossens (oboe) and Orchestra, conducted by Neils Gron

1932

Adieu
for solo piano
First performance: unable to trace
Keith Prowse, 1933

Funeral March: F. Chopin from *Piano Sonata in Bb minor, Op.35*
Arranged for orchestra
2+1.2+1.2+1.2+1/4.3.3.1/timp./perc./harp/strings
First performance (H.M.V. recording session): London, Abbey Road
30 May 1932
B.B.C. Symphony Orchestra, conducted by Adrian Boult
Unpublished

Impromptu
for solo piano
'Evelyn Frances Barron Dales'
Unpublished

Mina
for small orchestra
1.1.2.2/2.2.2.0/timp./perc./strings

'Fred Gaisberg'
First performance: London, E.M.I. recording Studio, 8 February 1934
The New Light Symphony Orchestra, conducted by J. Ainslie Murray
Keith Prowse, 1934

The Rapid Stream
Unison or two-part song for chorus and piano
Text: C.Mackay (1814–1889)
Keith Prowse, 1932

Serenade
for solo piano
'John Austin, friend and editor for many years'
Keith Prowse, 1933

So many true princesses who have gone
Ode for mixed chorus and military band
Text: John Masefield (1875–1967)
First performance: London, Marlborough House, 8 June 1932
Choirs from the Chapel Royal and Westminster Abbey with the band of
The Welsh Guards, conducted by Edward Elgar
(The unveiling of the memorial to Queen Alexandra)

When Swallows Fly
Unison or two-part song for chorus and piano
Text: C. Mackay (1814–1889)
'Stephen S. Moore'
First performance: Worcester, 18 May 1933
Keith Prowse, 1933

The Woodland Stream
Unison or two-part song for chorus and piano
Text: C.Mackay (1814–1889)
'Stephen S.Moore, Worcester'
First performance: Worcester, 18 May 1933
Keith Prowse, 1932

1933

Concerto for Piano and Orchestra (Op.90)
Incomplete

The Spanish Lady
Opera in two acts
Libretto by Barry Jackson (1879–1961) after Ben Jonson (1573–1637)
Incomplete
A concert performance of *The Spanish Lady* was given on 15 May 1986 in St. John's, Smith Square, London by the City University Symphony Orchestra and soloists from the Guildhall School of Music, conducted by Colin Masur.
The opera has now been 'reconstructed' by Dr. Percy Young and was performed on 24 November 1994 at the Cambridge Elgar Festival
Elkin [1955]: *Two Songs*
Elkin 1956: *Suite for String Orchestra*
Elkin 1958: *Sarabande and Bouree*

Symphony No.3 in C minor (Op.88)
Commissioned by the BBC
Incomplete

Tarantella
Song for baritone and orchestra
Text: Hilaire Belloc (1870–1953)
Incomplete

Recordings

of Elgar conducting his own works

Recordings are arranged chronologically by date of recording under each
title.

The Banner of St. George (Op.33)
    Epilogue: 'It Comes from the Misty Ages'
    Philharmonic Choir and London Symphony Orchestra
    in RLS 713
        CDS 7 545642
    Recorded 3 February 1928 in Queen's Hall, London

Bavarian Dances (Op.27)
    Nos. 2 and 3
    Symphony Orchestra
    in D 175–6
        GEM 113
        GEMM CD 9952
    Recorded 26 June 1914 at H.M.V. Studios, Hayes, Middlesex

    No.1
    Symphony Orchestra
    in D 175
        GEM 113
        GEMM CD 9952
    Recorded 28 February 1917 at H.M.V. Studios, Hayes,
    Middlesex

Nos.1 and 2
London Symphony Orchestra
in D 1367
    HLM 7005
    RLS 713
    CDS 7 545642
Recorded 15 July 1927 in Queen's Hall, London

No.3
London Symphony Orchestra
in DB 1667
    DB 7151
    HLM 7005
    RLS 713
    CD 7 545642
Recorded 4 February 1932 at E.M.I.'s No.1 Studio, Abbey
Road, London

Beau Brummel: Minuet
London Symphony Orchestra
in D 1638
    D 7486
    RLS 713
    CDS 7 54568 2
Recorded 13 June 1928 in Kingsway Hall, London

Carillon (Op.75)
Henry Ainley (reciter) and Symphony Orchestra
in D 177
    GEM 112
    EWE 1
  GEMM CD 9951
Recorded 15 January 1915 at H.M.V. Studios, Hayes, Middlesex

Carissima
Symphony Orchestra
in D 176
    GEM 111
    EWE 1

GEMM CD 9951
Recorded 21 January 1914 at H.M.V. Studios, Hayes, Middlesex
New Symphony Orchestra
in E 547
    RLS 713
Recorded 6 November 1929 in Small Queen's Hall, London

Chanson de Matin (Op.15 no.2)
London Symphony Orchestra
in D 1236
    HLM 7005
    RLS 713
    CDS 7 54564 2
Recorded 1 April 1927 in Queen's Hall, London

Chanson de Nuit (Op.15 no.1)
Symphony Orchestra
in D 180
    GEM 113
    EWE 1
  GEMM CD 9953
Recorded 22 May 1919 at H.M.V. Studios, Hayes, Middlesex

Royal Albert Hall Orchestra
in D 1236
    HLM 7005
    RLS 713
    CDS 7 54564 2
Recorded 27 April 1926 in Queen's Hall, London

Civic Fanfare
London Symphony Orchestra
in RLS 708
    SH 175
    CDS 7 54560 2
Recorded 4 September 1927 at the opening service of the
Three Choirs Festival in Hereford Cathedral

Cockaigne (Op.40)
>
> Symphony Orchestra
> *in* D 178 (abridged)
>> GEM 110
>> GEMM CD 9952
>
> Recorded 28 February 1917 at H.M.V. Studios, Hayes, Middlesex
>
> Royal Albert Hall Orchestra
> *in* D1110–11
>> RLS 713
>> CDS 7 54568 2
>
> Recorded 27 April 1926 in Queen's Hall, London
>
> BBC Symphony Orchestra
> *in* DB 1935–36
>> ALP 1464
>> RLS 713
>> BBC 4001
>> CDS 7 54568 2
>
> Recorded 11 April 1933 in E.M.I.'s No. 1 Studio, Abbey Road, London

Concerto for Cello and Orchestra (Op.85)
>
> Beatrice Harrison (cello) and Symphony Orchestra
> *in* D 541 and 545 (1st and 4th movements)
>> GEM 113
>> GEMM CD 9953
>
> Recorded 22 December 1919 at H.M.V. Studios, Hayes, Middlesex
>
> Beatrice Harrison (cello) and the New Symphony Orchestra
> *in* D 1507–9
>> D 7455–7
>> RLS 708
>> SH 175
>> CDS 7 54568 2
>
> Recorded 23 March and 13 June 1928 in Kingsway Hall, London

Concerto for Violin and Orchestra (Op.61)
Marie Hall (violin) and Symphony Orchestra
in D 79–80
    GEM 112
    GEMM CD 9952
Recorded 16 December 1916 at H.M.V. Studios, Hayes,
Middlesex

Yehudi Menuhin (violin) and the London Symphony Orchestra
in DB 1751–6
    DB 7175–80
    ALP 1456
    RLS 708
    HLM 7107
    CDS 7 54564 2
Recorded 14 and 15 July 1932 at E.M.I.'s No. 1 Studio, Abbey
Road, London

Contrasts: The Gavotte (Three Characteristic Pieces, Op.10)
London Philharmonic Orchestra
in DB 1910
    DB 2133
    DB 7403
    RLS 713
    CDS 7 54564 2
Recorded 21 February 1933 at E.M.I.'s No. 1 Studio, Abbey
Road, London

Crown of India: Suite (Op.66)
London Symphony Orchestra
in D 1899–1900
    RLS 713
    CDS 7 54564 2
Recorded 15 September and 22 November 1930 in Kingsway Hall,
London

The Dream of Gerontius (Op.38)
'Prelude' and 'Angel's Farewell' (abridged)
in D 181
    GEM 111
  GEMM CD 9952
Recorded 28 February 1917 at H.M.V. Studios, Hayes,
Middlesex

Extracts with soloists, Royal Choral Society and Royal
Albert Hall Orchestra
in D 1242–43
    HLM 7009
    RLS 713
    CDS 7 54560 2
Recorded 26 February 1927 at a performance in the Royal
Albert Hall, London

Extracts with soloists, Three Choirs Festival Chorus and
London Symphony Orchestra
in D 1348 and 1350
    HLM 7009
    RLS 708
    SH 175
Recorded 6 September 1927 at a performance in Hereford
Cathedral

Elegy for Strings (Op.58)
London Philharmonic Orchestra
in DB 1939
    RLS 713
    CDS 7 54568 2
Recorded 29 August 1933 at E.M.I.'s No.1 Studio, Abbey Road,
London

Falstaff (Op.68)
Two Interludes
New Symphony Orchestra
in D 1863
    RLS 713
    CDS 7 54568 2

Recorded 8 November 1929 in Small Queen's Hall, London
London Symphony Orchestra (with W.H. Reed, solo violin)
in DB 1621–4
> DB 7112–5
> BLP 1090
> SH 162
> RLS 708
> CDS 7 54560 2

Recorded 11 and 12 November 1931 and 4 February 1932 at
E.M.I.'s No. 1 Studio, Abbey Road, London

Fantasia and Fugue in C minor (Op.86): Bach, arr. Elgar
Fugue
Royal Albert Hall Orchestra
in D 614
> GEM 115
> EWE 1
> GEMM CD 9955

Recorded 7 December 1921 at H.M.V. Studios, Hayes, Middlesex

Fantasia
Royal Albert Hall Orchestra
in D 638
> GEM 115
> EWE 1
> GEMM CD 9955

Recorded 26 October 1923 at H.M.V. Studios, Hayes, Middlesex

Fantasia and Fugue
Royal Albert Hall Orchestra
in W 749
> RLS 708
> HLM 7107
> CDS 7 54564 2

Recorded 28 April 1926 in Queen's Hall, London

Fringes of the Fleet
Soloists and Orchestra
in D 453–454
GEM 112
EWE 1
GEMM CD 9952
Recorded 28 February 1917 at H.M.V. Studios, Hayes,
Middlesex

Froissart (Op.19)
London Philharmonic Orchestra
in DB 1938–39
RLS 713
CDS 7 54568 2
Recorded 21 February 1933 at E.M.I's No.1 Studio, Abbey
Road, London

God save the King: arr. Elgar
Philharmonic Choir and London Symphony Orchestra
in C 1467
RLS 713
CDS 7 54564 2
Recorded 3 February 1928 in Queen's Hall, London

In the South (Op.50)
Royal Albert Hall Orchestra
in D 785–86
GEM 115
EWE 1
GEMM CD 9954
Recorded 30 December 1921 and 26 October 1923 at H.M.V.
Studios, Hayes, Middlesex

London Symphony Orchestra
in D 1666–67
DB 7151-3
RLS 713
CDS 7 54568 2
Recorded 18 September 1930 in Kingsway Hall, London

King Olaf (Op.30)
'A Little Bird in the Air' (arr. for orchestra by Elgar)
Royal Albert Hall Orchestra
in D 614
  GEM 114
  GEMM CD 9954
Recorded 7 December 1921 at H.M.V. Studios, Hayes, Middlesex

The Kingdom (Op.51)
Prelude
B.B.C. Symphony Orchestra
in DB 1934
  SH 139
  RLS 708
  CDS 7 54568 2
Recorded 11 April 1933 at E.M.I.'s No.1 Studio, Abbey Road,
London

Land of Hope and Glory
Margaret Balfour (contralto), Philharmonic Chorus and London
Symphony Orchestra
in C 1467
  RLS 713
  CDS 7 54564 2
Recorded 3 February 1928 in Queen's Hall, London

Light of Life (Op.29)
'Meditation'
Royal Albert Hall Orchestra
in D 1017
  GEM 116
  EWE 1
  GEMM CD 9955
Recorded 16 April 1925 at H.M.V. Studios, Hayes, Middlesex

Royal Albert Hall Orchestra
in D 1157
  D 7149

D 7564
RLS 713
CDS 7 54564 2
Recorded 30 August 1926 in Queen's Hall, London

May Song
New Symphony Orchestra
in D 1949
D 7316
D 7620
CDS 7 54568 2
Recorded 7 November 1929 in Small Queen's Hall, London

Mazurka (Three Characteristic Pieces, Opus 10)
New Symphony Orchestra
in JF 38
HLM 7005
RLS 713
CDS 7 54564 2
Recorded 8 November 1929 in Small Queen's Hall, London

Minuet (Op.21)
New Symphony Orchestra
in D 1863
RLS 713
CDS 7 54568 2
Recorded 8 November 1929 in Small Queen's Hall, London

The Music Makers (Op.69)
Excerpts with soloists, Three Choirs Festival Chorus,
Herbert Brewer (organ) and the London Symphony Orchestra
in D 1347 and 1349
SH 175
RLS 708
CDS 7 54560 2
Recorded 8 September 1927 at a performance in Hereford
Cathedral

Nursery Suite
London Symphony Orchestra (with W.H.Reed, violin and Gordon
Walker, flute)
in D 1998–99
> RLS 713
> CDS 7 54564 2

Recorded 23 May and 4 June 1931 in Kingsway Hall, London

Overture in D minor: Handel, arr. Elgar
Royal Albert Hall Orchestra
in D 838
> GEM 115
> EWE 1
> GEMM CD 9955

Recorded 26 October 1923 in H.M.V.'s Studios, Hayes,
Middlesex

Polonia (Op.76)
Symphony Orchestra
in D 493
> GEM 113
> EWE 1
> GEMM CD 9953

Recorded 22 May 1919 in H.M.V.'s Studios, Hayes, Middlesex

Pomp and Circumstance Military Marches (Op.39)
Nos. 1 and 4
Symphony Orchestra
in D 179
> GEM 110
> EWE 1
> GEMM CD 9951

Recorded 26 June 1914 at H.M.V.'s Studios, Hayes, Middlesex

Nos. 1 and 2
Royal Albert Hall Orchestra
in D 1102
> RLS 713

CDS 7 54568 2
Recorded 27 April 1926 in Queen's Hall, London

Nos. 3 and 4
London Symphony Orchestra
in D 1301
    HLM 7005 (No.3 only)
    RLS 713
    CDS 7 54568 2
Recorded 15 July 1927 in Queen's Hall, London

No.5
London Symphony Orchestra
in D 1900
    HLM 7005
    RLS 713
    CDS 7 54568 2
Recorded 18 September 1930 in Kingsway Hall, London

No. 1 (Trio: 'Land of Hope and Glory')
London Symphony Orchestra (with introduction by Elgar)
in RLS 713
    CDS 7 54568 2

Nos. 1 and 2 (both cut)
B.B.C. Symphony Orchestra with Berkeley Mason (organ)
in DB 1801
    HLM 7005
    RLS 713
    CDS 7 54568 2
Recorded 7 October 1932 in Kingsway Hall, London

No. 4
B.B.C. Symphony Orchestra
in DB 1936
    HLM 7005
    RLS 713

Recorded 11 April 1933 at E.M.I.'s No.1 Studio, Abbey Road, London

Rosemary
New Symphony Orchestra
in D 1778
    RLS 713
    CDS 7 54568 2
Recorded 7 November 1929 in Small Queen's Hall, London

Salut d'Amour
Symphony Orchestra
in D 180
    GEM 110
    GEMM CD 9951
Recorded 26 June 1914 at H.M.V.'s Studios, Hayes, Middlesex

New Symphony Orchestra
in E 547
    HLM 7005
    RLS 713
    CDS 7 54568 2
Recorded 8 November 1929 in Small Queen's Hall, London

The Sanguine Fan (Op.81)
Selection
Symphony Orchestra
in D 596
    GEM 114
    EWE 1
    GEMM CD 9953
Recorded 24 February 1920 at H.M.V.'s Studios, Hayes, Middlesex

Sea Pictures (Op.37)
Leila Megane (contralto) and Royal Albert Hall Orchestra
in D 674 and 675
    GEM 115
    EWE 1

GEMM CD 9954

Recorded 10 November 1922 and 8 January 1923 at H.M.V.'s Studios, Hayes, Middlesex

Serenade for Strings (Op.20)

London Philharmonic Orchestra

in DB 2132–33

    ALP 1464

    RLS 713

    CDS 7 54568 2

Recorded 29 August 1933 in E.M.I.'s No.1 Studio, Abbey Road, London

Sérénade Lyrique

New Symphony Orchestra

in D 1778

    RLS 713

    CDS 7 54568 2

Recorded 6 November 1929 in Small Queen's Hall, London

Sérénade Mauresque (Three Characteristic Pieces, Op.10)

New Symphony Orchestra

in HMV matrix CC18153

    CDS 7 54564 2 (previously unpublished)

Recorded 8 November 1929 in Small Queen's Hall, London

Severn Suite (Op.87)

London Symphony Orchestra

in DB 1908–1910

    DB 7403–7405

    RLS 713

    CDS 7 54564 2

Recorded 14 April 1932 at E.M.I.'s No.1 Studio, Abbey Road, London

Starlight Express (Op.78)

Excerpts with soloists and Symphony Orchestra

in D 455–458

    GEM 111

    GEMM CD 9951

Recorded 18 February 1918 at H.M.V.'s Studio, Hayes,
Middlesex

Symphony No.1 (Op.55)
London Symphony Orchestra
in D 1944–49
    D 7311–16
    D 7620 25
    SH 139
    RLS 708
    CDS 7 54560 2
Recorded 20,21 and 22 November 1930 in Kingsway Hall, London

Symphony No.2 (Op.63)
Royal Albert Hall Orchestra
in D 1012–17
    GEM 116
    EWE 1
  GEMM CD 9955
Recorded 1 and 20 March 1924 at H.M.V.'s Studios, Hayes,
Middlesex

London Symphony Orchestra
in D 1230–35
    D 7239–44
    D 7558–63
    SH 163
    RLS 708
    CDS 7 54560 2
Recorded 1 April and 15 July 1927 in Queen's Hall, London

Variations on an Original Theme ('Enigma') (Op.36)
Symphony Orchestra
in D 578, 582, 596, 602
    GEM 114
    EWE 1
  GEMM CD 9954
Recorded 24 February and 16 November 1920, and 11 May 1921
at H.M.V.'s Studios, Hayes, Middlesex

Royal Albert Hall Orchestra
in D 1154–57
    D 7564–67
    ALP 1464
    SH 162
    RLS 708
    CDS 7 54564 2
Recorded 28 April 1926 in Queen's Hall, London

Wand of Youth Suite No.1
Symphony Orchestra
in D 468
    GEM 110
    GEMM CD 9953
Recorded 22 May 1919 at H.M.V.'s Studios, Hayes, Middlesex

London Symphony Orchestra
in D 1636–38
    D 7486–90
    RLS 713
    CDS 7 54564 2
Recorded 19 December 1928 in Kingsway Hall, London

Wand of Youth Suite No.2
Excerpts
Symphony Orchestra
in D 178
    GEM 110
    GEMM CD 9953
Recorded 28 February 1917 at H.M.V.'s Studios, Hayes, Middlesex

Excerpts
London Symphony Orchestra
in D 1649–50
    D 7486–90
    RLS 713
    CDS 7 54564 2
Recorded 20 December 1928 in Kingsway Hall, London

Collections

The Athenaeum Library, London

Manuscript sketches: Symphony No. 2 (Op.63)

E. Wulstan Atkins, Woldingham, Surrey

Correspondence

Baillieu Library (University of Melbourne)

Correspondence

Barber Institute (University of Birmingham)

Correspondence
Manuscripts: The Music Makers (Op.69)

British Broadcasting Corporation Written Archives, Caversham

Correspondence: the commissioning of Symphony No.3 (Op.88)

Birmingham Oratory

Manuscripts: Full score of The Dream of Gerontius (Op.38)

The Bodleian Library, Oxford

Correspondence
Manuscripts: Full score of The Kingdom (Op.51)

Boston Public Library (U.S.A.)

Correspondence

British Library (London): Department of Manuscripts

Correspondence
Manuscripts: One of the important core collections acquired by deposit
and subsequent purchase

Central Music Library, London

Correspondence: Between Elgar and Edwin Evans

Charnwood Borough Council

Manuscripts: Memorial Chimes for a Carillon (Loughborough)

Elgar Birthplace, Lower Broadheath, Worcester

Books, documents, letters, manuscripts and memorabilia

FitzWilliam Museum, Cambridge

Manuscripts: Full score of Falstaff (Op.68)

Gentleman: Co. Kerry (Eire)

Manuscript: Arrangement of Carafa aria (1879)

Glasgow City Libraries

Correspondence

Gloucester City Libraries

Manuscripts: Elgar's orchestration of Herbert Brewer's cantata 'Emmaus'
(1901)

Hereford and Worcester Record Office

Letters, postcards, telegrams and other papers written by Elgar and
members of his family

Hereford Cathedral Library

Manuscripts: The Moods of Dan (1897, 1898, 1902 and 1903)
Working sketches of In the South (Op.50)
Vocal Score of A Christmas Greeting (Op.52)
Sketches for The Crown of India (Op.66)

Houghton Library (Harvard University, U.S.A.)

Correspondence: Between Elgar and William Rothenstein
Manuscripts: Full score of May Song (1901)

Humanities Research Center (HRC), University of Texas at Austin

Printed score of the Severn Suite, annotated by George Bernard Shaw

Leeds City Libraries

Correspondence

Library of Congress, Washington, DC, U.S.A.

Correspondence
Manuscripts: Sketches of the Violin Concerto (Op.61)

Manchester City Libraries

Correspondence

Raymond Monk, Leicester

Correspondence: Fred Gaisberg; John West; G.B. Shaw, etc.

The Elgar Diaries

Proof copy: Symphony No.2 (Op.63)
Sketches: The Dream of Gerontius (Op.38)

Music Library, Northwestern University, Evanston, U.S.A.

Correspondence including letters to Rosa Burley

Manuscripts: many of the early works for wind quintet,
                including
                Harmony Music Nos. 1,2,3,4,5,6
                Evesham Andante
                Promenade Nos. 1,2,3,4,5,6
                Andante Cantabile (Mrs Winslow's Soothing Syrup)
                Menuetto in Bb
                Sarabande
                Gigue
                Five Intermezzi, together with
                In Smyrna
                Four Part Songs (Op.53), fair copy of No.4

Oliver Neighbour, London

Manuscripts: Sketches of Froissart (Op.19)

**Percival Price Collection (Music Division) National Library of
    Canada, Ottawa**

Manuscripts: Land of Hope and Glory (1902) – Carillon obbligato
for chorus (arranged 1927)

Keith Prowse Ltd., London

Manuscripts: orchestral parts of the Civic Fanfare (1927)

Public Archives of Canada, Ottawa

Correspondence and part manuscript of Carillon (Op.75)

Royal Academy of Music, London

Correspondence

Manuscripts: Full score of In the South (Op.50)
                Copy of The Crown of India Suite (Op. 66)
                Full score of Overture in D minor (Handel)

Royal College of Music, London

Correspondence

Dorabella Archive (Mrs Dora Powell): includes miscellaneous papers, correspondence, lecture notes, newspaper cuttings, photographs, music by Elgar (and others) with particular reference to the *Enigma Variations*, from the estate of Mrs Dora Powell. Presented by Mr. and Mrs Claud Powell, 1986

Manuscripts: The Black Knight (Op.25): Full score
The Shepherd's Song (Op.16 no.1)
Rondel (Op. 16 no. 3)
The Banner of St.George: epilogue, arr. for band
God Save the King (1902): arr. for band
The Kingdom (Op.51): The Lord's Prayer (V.S.)
Elegy (Op.58): proofs
The Starlight Express (Op.78): A Song of Laughter
Cello Concerto (Op. 85): Full score
With Proud Thanksgiving: arr. for band
It isnae me (1930): sketch and proofs
Chopin's Funeral March, orchestrated: Full score

Royal Library, Windsor Castle

Manuscripts: O Hearken Thou (Op.64) – Full score
Queen Alexandra Memorial Ode – Short score

Sibelius Museum, Turku, Finland

Correspondence

Stanford University (U.S.A.), Music Library

Manuscripts: Salut d'amour (Op.12)
Enigma Variations (Op.36): piano score
Violin Concerto: proofs

Stiftelsen Musikkulturens framjande, Stockholm, Sweden

Manuscripts: Four Part-songs (Op.53) – Fair copies of nos.2 and 3

Trinity College Library, Cambridge

Correspondence

University of Bristol Library

Correspondence

University of Cambridge Library

Correspondence: from Elgar to Arthur Bliss

Manuscripts: Angelus (Tuscany): from Arthur Bliss's Library
The Kingdom: proofs and autographed corrections

University of Edinburgh Library

Correspondence

University of London Library

Correspondence

University of Manchester Library

Correspondence

Worcester Cathedral Library

Manuscripts: Froissart (Op.19): copy

Worshipful Company of Musicians, London

Manuscripts: Elegy (Op.58): Full score

Yale University Library (U.S.A.)

Correspondence

Select Bibliography

This select bibliography presents writings relating to Edward Elgar and his music from the earliest years to the present day.

All articles, books, theses, record reviews and sleeve notes, together with programme notes, are arranged under the relevant headings of Elgar's works if they are specifically concerned with those works. The category GENERAL deals mainly with biographical aspects of the composer's life and general mention of his works. All items are listed in alphabetical order of author's name.

THE APOSTLES (Op. 49)

ANDERSON, R. 'Elgar and some apostolic problems', *Musical Times* 125 (January 1984), pp. 13–15

ANON. [The Apostles], *Musical Opinion* 80 (August 1957), pp. 647+

ANON. 'The Apostles in New York', *Musical Times* 45 (April 1904), p. 237

ANON. 'The Birmingham Music Festival', *Musical Times* 44 (November 1903), pp. 725–27

ANON. 'Occasional notes: second performance of The Apostles in New York', *Musical Times* 44 (May 1904), p. 304

ANON. [Review of the Berlin performance quoting German press comments], *Musical Times* 47 (April 1906), p. 243

ANON. [Review of English performances], *Musical Times* 44 (November 1903), p. 720

ANON. [Review of the New York performances quoting the Brooklyn Eagle], *Musical Times* 48 (May 1907), p. 307

BAUGHAN, E.A. 'The Apostles and Elgar's future' *in Music and Musicians*, London, John Lane, 1906

BISHOP, C. 'Elgar's Apostles', *The Listener* 87 (22 June 1972), p. 842

BLACKBURN, V. 'The Apostles', *Musical Times* 44 (July 1903), pp. 449–451

BONAVIA, F. 'Elgar's The Apostles', *Musical Times* 85 (December 1944), pp. 378–79

CROSS, A. 'Birmingham', *Musical Times* 115 (November 1974), p. 968

[EDWARDS, F.G.] 'Dr. Elgar's new oratorio The Apostles: an interview with the composer', *Musical Times* 44 (April 1903), pp. 228–29

G.-F,C. [The Apostles], *Musical Opinion* 80 (August 1957), p. 647

GORTON, C.V. 'The Apostles: an interpretation of the libretto', London, Novello, 1903

GORTON, C.V. 'Dr. Elgar's oratorio The Apostles', *Musical Times* 44 (October 1903), pp. 656–57

GROGAN, C. 'The Apostles: Some Thoughts on the Early Plans' *in* 'Edward Elgar: Music and Literature' (ed. Raymond Monk) Aldershot, Scolar Press, 1993

GROGAN, C. 'Elgar's rejected apostle', *Musical Times* 129 (February 1988), pp. 70–74

GROGAN, C. 'My dear analyst: some observations on Elgar's correspondence with A.J.Jaeger regarding the Apostles project' *Music and Letters* 72 (January 1991), pp. 48–60

GROGAN, C. 'A study of Elgar's creative processes in The Apostles (Op. 49) with particular reference to Scene II: By the Wayside' Ph.D. thesis, University of London, 1989

HODGKINS, G. 'Prisoners of hope: Sir Adrian Boult's recording of The Apostles' *Elgar Society Journal* 6 (September 1989), pp. 13–18

JAEGER, A.J. 'The Apostles: book of words with analytical notes and descriptive notes' London, Novello, 1903

KENNEDY, M. 'The Apostles' *Gramophone* 66 (September 1988), pp. 460+65

KENNEDY, M. Sleeve note for CMS7 49742–2 (1988)

KENNEDY, M. Sleeve note for SLS 976 (1974)

KEYS, I. 'The Apostles: Elgar and Bach as Preachers' *in* 'Edward Elgar: Music and Literature' (ed. Raymond Monk) Aldershot, Scolar Press, 1993

KIRBY, A.J. 'The Apostles and The Kingdom' *in* 'Edward Elgar: Centenary Sketches' (ed. H.A.Chambers) London, Novello, 1957

MARKSON, L. 'Elgar's Apostles', *Records and Recordings* 18 (November 1974), pp. 18–19

MOORE, J.N. 'Aberdeenshire', *Musical Times* 116 (July 1975), p. 648

MOORE, J.N 'The Apostles', *Gramophone* 52 (November 1974), pp. 936+41

MOORE, J.N. 'Elgar's Apostles: the project of a lifetime', *Gramophone* 52 (November 1974), pp. 877–78

NAGLEY, J. 'Elgar, Bruckner', *Musical Times* 120 (January 1979), p. 59

PAYNE, A. 'Gerontius apart', *Music and Musicians* 13 (December 1964), pp. 25+49

POWELL, D.M. 'The first performances of The Apostles and The Kingdom', *Musical Times* 101 (January 1960), pp. 21–22

POWELL, D.M. 'The words of The Apostles and The Kingdom', *Musical Times* (Part 1) 89 (July 1948), pp. 201–4; (Part 2) 90 (May 1949), pp. 149–52

RUSHTON, J. 'Records: The Apostles', *Music and Musicians* 23 (January 1975), pp. 36+38

ARRANGEMENTS AND TRANSCRIPTIONS OF MUSIC BY OTHER COMPOSERS

Bach, J.S.

C minor Organ Fantasia, transcribed for orchestra
THOMPSON, H. 'The Gloucester Music Festival', *Musical Times* 63 (October 1922), pp. 705–8

C minor Organ Fugue, transcribed for orchestra
GRACE, H. 'The Bach-Elgar Fugue', *Musical Times* 63 (January 1922), pp. 21–23
GRACE, H. 'London concerts: L.S.O. first performance of Elgar's arrangement', *Musical Times* 62 (December 1921), p. 846
ROSEN, C. [Fugue in C minor] *in* 'The Goossens: a musical century', London, Deutsch, 1993
St. Matthew Passion: edition arranged with Ivor Atkins
ANON. 'Occasional notes: criticisms', *Musical Times* 64 (May 1923), p. 332
ANON. 'Worcester Music Festival', *Musical Times* 52 (October 1911), pp. 665–67
BLYTH, A. 'St. Matthew Passion', *Gramophone* 56 (March 1979), p. 1594
HUNT, B. 'St. Matthew Passion', *Daily Telegraph* (Arts), 2 April 1994, p. 16
WILLCOCKS, D. Sleeve notes for QSS 324 (1994)

Battishall, J.

O Lord look down
THOMPSON, H. 'The Worcester Festival', *Musical Times* 64 (October 1923), pp. 715–17

Brewer, H.

Emmaus
BROWN, D.J. 'Emmaus', Programme note for the performance at the Gloucester Three Choirs Festival, 28 August 1992
TROTT, M. 'Elgar's orchestration of Brewer's Emmaus', *Elgar Society Journal* 3 (January 1984), pp. 26–30

Chopin, F.

Funeral March
MOORE, J.N. 'Chopin's Funeral March (orchestrated Elgar)', *Gramophone* 52 (February 1975), p. 1491

Handel, G.F.

Overture in D minor
ANON. 'Occasional notes', *Musical Times* 64 (October 1923), pp. 712–13

Parry, C.H.H.

THOMPSON, H. 'The Leeds Music Festival', *Musical Times* 63 (November 1922), pp. 796–98

Wesley, S.S.

THOMPSON, H. 'The Worcester Festival', *Musical Times* 64 (October 1923), pp. 715–17

ARTHUR: Incidental music for the play

ANDERSON, R. 'fyrst the noble Arthur' *in* 'Edward Elgar: Music and Literature' (ed. Raymond Monk) Aldershot, Scolar Press, 1993
BONAVIA, F. 'Elgar's music to Binyon's Arthur', *Musical Times* 64 (April 1923), p. 272
WIMBUSH, R. 'Here and There', *Gramophone* 51 (August 1973), pp. 326–28
See also under *King Arthur*

THE BANNER OF ST. GEORGE (Op. 33)

ANON. 'Let the people sing', *Musical Opinion* 80 (June 1957), p. 517
ANON. 'Reviews', *Musical Times* 38 (May 1897), p. 318
KENNEDY, M. 'The Banner of St. George', *Gramophone* 64 (March 1987), pp. 1309–10
MOORE, J.N. Sleeve note for CDC7 47658–2 (1987)

BEAU BRUMMEL: Incidental music for the play

BONAVIA, F. 'Elgar's music to Beau Brummel', *Musical Times* 69 (December 1928), p. 1124
HARVEY, T. 'Beau Brummel', *Gramophone* 42 (October 1964), p. 182
WELDON, H., etc. Sleeve note for CLP 1766/CSD 1555 (1964)

THE BLACK KNIGHT (Op. 25)

ANON. 'A Local Composer's Triumph', *Worcester Daily Times*, 19 April 1893
ANON. 'Elgarian Groves', *Gramophone* 62 (November 1984), p. 568
KENNEDY, M. 'The Black Knight', *Gramophone* 62 (May 1985), p. 1364
McVEAGH, D. 'Sibelius, Kajanus, Elgar', *Musical Times* 116 (April 1975), pp. 357–58
McVEAGH, D. 'Sullivan, Elgar,' *Musical Times* 120 (January 1979), p. 59

POPE, M. Sleeve note for CDC7 47511–2 (1987)
POPE, M. Sleeve note for EL 270157–1 (1985)
SANDERS, A. 'The Black Knight', *Gramophone* 65 (August 1987), p. 338

CARACTACUS (Op. 35)

ANON. 'Editorial Notes', *Strad* 85 (January 1975), pp. 533–34
ANON. 'Here and There', *Gramophone* 54 (August 1976), p. 271
ANON. 'Nostalgia?', *Musical Opinion* 93 (October 1969), pp. 5–6
ANON. [Review of publications], *Musical Times* 40 (July 1899), p. 478
BAUGHAN, E.A. [Caractacus: Review], *Musical Standard* 1 October 1898, p. 210
    8 October 1898, pp. 226–27
DOMMETT, K. 'Anglo-American Cheltenham', *Music and Musicians* 19
    September 1970, pp. 28–29+82
GREENFIELD, E. 'Caractacus', *Gramophone* 55 (June 1977), p. 84
HOLLAND, A.K. 'Elgar's Caractacus as opera', *Musical Times* 69 (February 1928),
    pp. 166–67
KENNEDY, M. Sleeve note for SLS 998 (1977)
LARNER, G. 'Cheltenham', *Musical Times* 111 (September 1970), p. 912
LOVELAND, K. 'Three Choirs', *Musical Times* 130 (November 1989), p. 700
McVEAGH, D. 'RPO/Fairfax', *Musical Times* 116 (February 1975), p. 161
MOORE, J.N. 'Caractacus: Triumphal March', *Gramophone* 52 (February 1975),
    p. 1491
PUFFETT, D. 'Radio', *Music and Musicians* 23 (January 1975), pp. 36–38
THOMPSON, H. 'Caractacus: book of words with analytical notes', London,
    Novello, 1900
WEBSTER, E.M. 'Cheltenham: the great cram-in', *Musical Opinion* 93 (September
    1970), p. 641

CARILLON (Op. 75)

COLLETT, B. Sleeve note for SHE CD 9602 (1988)
KEETON, A.E. 'The Binyon-Elgar Carillon 1941' *Musical Times* 84 (March 1943),
    p. 92
KEETON, A.E. 'The Binyon-Elgar Carillon 1941', *Musical Times* 84 (April 1943),
    p. 123
KENNEDY, M. Sleeve note for ASD 3050 (1975)
KENNEDY, M. Sleeve note for CDM7 69207–2 (1988)
MOORE, J.N 'Carillon', *Gramophone* 52 (February 1975), p. 1491
SANDERS, A. 'Carillon', *Gramophone* 65 (April 1988), p. 1500
SANDERS, A. 'Carillon', *Gramophone* 65 (May 1988), p. 1628

CARISSIMA

ANON. 'Gramophone notes', *Strad* 80 (January 1970), p. 437

CHANSON DE MATIN

ANON. [Review of the arrangement for military band], *Musical Times* 42 (September 1901), p. 614

ANON. [Review of publication], *Musical Times* 41 (October 1900), p. 675

ANON. [Review of publication: arrangement for viola and piano], *Musical Times* 42 (March 1901), p. 185

CIVIC FANFARE

CHISLETT, W.A 'Civic Fanfare', *Gramophone* 55 (June 1977), pp. 67–68

GOODWIN, N. Sleeve note for CHAN 6573 (1991)

COCKAIGNE (In London Town) (Op. 40)

ANDERSON, W.R. 'Cockaigne', *Gramophone* 28 (December 1950), p. 141

ANON. 'Dr. Elgar's new overture', *Musical Times* 42 (July 1901), p. 472

HARVEY, T. 'Cockaigne', *Gramophone* 32 (April 1955), p. 481

HURD, M. 'Elgar: Cockaigne', *Music in Education* 38 (1974), pp. 119–121

SANDERS, A. 'Cockaigne', *Gramophone* 66 (December 1988), p. 1072

CONCERT ALLEGRO

ANON. 'The story of a lost manuscript', *Musical Opinion* 92 (February 1969), pp. 229–230

ANON. 'Unpublished Elgar manuscript re-discovered', *Musical Events* 24 (February 1969), pp. 34–35

McVEAGH, D. 'Elgar's Concert Allegro', *Musical Times* 110 (February 1969), pp. 135–38

MASON, E. 'Ogdon's Elgar', *Music and Musicians* 17 (March 1969), p. 48

CONCERTO FOR PIANO AND ORCHESTRA (Op. 90)

ANON. 'Elgar's Piano Concerto', *Music and Musicians* 27 (March 1979), p. 21

ANON. 'Harriet Cohen, Boyd Neel Orchestra and Walter Goehr', *Musical Opinion* 79 (March 1956), p. 328

MITCHELL, D. 'Some first performances', *Musical Times* 97 (March 1956), p. 149

CONCERTO FOR VIOLIN AND ORCHESTRA (Op. 61)

ANON. [Concerto for Violin and Orchestra], New York Philharmonic Symphony Society Program Notes, 12 January 1950

ANON. 'M.Ysaÿe and the Elgar Violin Concerto', *Musical Times* 54 (January 1913), pp. 19–20

ANON. 'Menuhin's Elgar: intimacy and bravura', *American Record Guide* 33 (September 1966), p. 38

ANON. 'Reviews', *Musical Opinion* 111 (October 1988), p. 357

APPLEBAUM, S. and S. 'Music in America', *Strad* 78 (February 1968), p. 403

BYARD, H. 'Edward Elgar (1857–1934)' *in* 'The Concerto' (ed. Ralph Hill), Harmondsworth, Penguin Book, 1952

CHAPIN, L. 'Menuhin's fortieth anniversary', *HiFi/Musical America* 18 (February 1968), p. MA14

COBBETT, W.W. 'Elgar's Violin Concerto', *Music Student* 8 (August 1916), pp. 368–372

GREENFIELD, E. 'A repeat performance at 50', *HiFi/Musical America* 16 (February 1966), pp. 24+

GREW, S. 'Elgar's Concerto for Violin and Orchestra', *Musical Opinion* 34 (July 1911), pp. 685–66; (August 1911), p. 761; (September 1911), p. 832

JACOBSON, B. 'Elgar's Violin Concerto: as played by Menuhin today and Menuhin yesterday', *HiFi/Musical America* 16 (September 1966), pp. 86–87

JONES,V. 'Helen Weaver, the Soul of Elgar's Violin Concerto', *Royal Academy of Music Magazine*, no.237 (1985), pp. 328+

KENNEDY, M. 'The Soul Enshrined:Elgar and his Violin Concerto' *in* 'Edward Elgar: Music and Literature' (ed. Raymond Monk), Aldershot, Scolar Press, 1993

MENUHIN, Y. 'Elgarian Authority', *Gramophone* 70 (February 1993), p. 13

MENUHIN, Y. Sleeve note for ALP 1456 (1957)

MENUHIN, Y. 'Some great musicians I have known – past & present', *Recorded Sound* no.48 (October 1972), pp. 98–108

NEWMAN, E. 'Elgar's Violin Concerto', *Musical Times* 51 (October 1910), pp. 631–34

PLANT, M. 'The Violin Concerto on record', *Elgar Society Newsletter* no.7 (September 1975), pp. 30–32

REED, N. 'Elgar's enigmatic Inamorata', *Musical Times* 125 (August 1984), pp. 430–34

REED, W.H. 'Elgar and his Violin Concerto', *The Listener*, 18 November 1937, p. 1042

REED, W.H. 'The Violin Concerto', *Music and Letters* 16 (January 1935), pp. 30–36

REES, C.B. 'Menuhin and Elgar's Violin Concerto', *Musical Events* 16 (November 1961), pp. 8–9

ROBERTSON, A. 'Concerto for Violin and Orchestra', *Gramophone* 35 (July 1957), p. 72

SANDERS, A. 'Concerto for Violin and Orchestra', *Gramophone* 67 (November 1989), p. 1010

SCHWARZ, K.R. 'Classical Review', *HiFi/Musical America* 36 (July 1986), p. 61

SHORE, B. 'Edward Elgar 1857–1934', *Gramophone* 35 (June 1957), p. 4

SMITH, H. 'Elgar from the East', *Gramophone* 71 (March 1994), pp. 16–17

TOVEY, D.F. 'Violin Concerto in B minor' *in* 'Essays in Musical Analysis': Volume 3 – Concertos London, Oxford University Press, 1936

WHITE, R.T. 'Elgar's Violin Concerto', *Music Student* 17 (January 1925), p. 51

CONCERTO FOR VIOLONCELLO AND ORCHESTRA (Op. 85)

ANDERSON, W.R. 'Concerto for Violoncello and Orchestra', *Gramophone* 28 (November 1950), pp. 111–112

ANON. 'The best Schelomo', *American Record Guide* 34 (January 1968), p. 375

ANON. 'Concerto for Violoncello and Orchestra (Op. 85)', *Houston Symphony Orchestra Program Notes* 5 November 1962, pp. 15+

ANON. 'Concerto for Violoncello and Orchestra', *National Symphony Orchestra Program Notes* 10 May 1967, p. 17

ANON. [Concerto for Violoncello and Orchestra Op. 85], *Pittsburgh Symphony Orchestra Program Notes* 25–27 April 1975, pp. 867–69

ANON. 'Elgar's Cello Concerto', *American Record Guide* 17 (October 1950), pp. 47–48

COLLES, H.C. 'Elgar's Violoncello Concerto', *Musical Times* 61 (February 1920), pp. 84–87

DALE, S. 'A great masterpiece: Elgar's Cello Concerto', *Strad* 80 (January 1970), pp. 409+

DENTON, D. 'The remains of the day', *Strad* 103 (September 1992), pp. 850,852,854

DUCHEN, J. 'Back to the Beginning', *Gramophone* 71 (June 1993), pp. 10 + 78

ELKIN, R. 'Elgar's Cello Concerto: an analysis', *Music in Education* 27 (no.304) 1963, pp. 185–87

GREENFIELD, E. 'Concerto for Violoncello and Orchestra', *Gramophone* 63 (May 1988), p. 1402

HARVEY, T. 'Concerto for Violoncello and Orchestra', *Gramophone* 43 (December 1965), p. 294

KALISCH, A. 'Elgar's new Violoncello Concerto', *Musical Times* 60 (December 1919), pp. 693–94

KEYS, I. 'Ghostly Stuff: The Brinkwells Music' *in* 'Edward Elgar: Music and Literature' (ed. Raymond Monk), Aldershot, Scolar Press, 1993

MOORE, J.N. Sleeve note for RLS 709 (April 1975)

MOORE,J.N. and BLYTH,A. Sleeve note for Testament SBT 2025 (1993)

POTTER, T. [Paul Tortellier and the Elgar Cello Concerto], Notes for Testament SBT 2025 (1993)

POTTER, T. 'Record Reviews', *Strad* 100 (July 1989), p. 589

STANFIELD, M.B. 'Some 'cellistic landmarks', *Strad* 60 (July 1949), pp. 90+; (August 1949), pp. 112+; (September 1949), pp. 148+; (November 1949), pp. 204+; Reprinted in *Violins* 14 (January–February 1953), pp. 26–7;

(Mar.–April 1953), pp. 75–76; (May–June 1953), pp. 130–131; (July–August 1953), pp. 172–3

TEACHOUT, T. 'Reviews', *HiFi/Musical America* 35 (December 1985), p. 68

TERTIS, L. [Cello Concerto – arranged for Viola] *in* 'Cinderella No More' London, Nevill, 1953; Reprinted in 'My Viola and I' London, Elek, 1974

WALSH, S. 'Concerto for Violoncello and Orchestra', *Gramophone* 52 (April 1975), pp. 1844+59

WYKES, D. 'Elgar's Cello Concerto: a query', *Musical Times* 101 (March 1960), pp. 156–57

CORONATION MARCH (Op. 65)

HARVEY, T. 'Coronation March (1911)', *Gramophone* 48 (April 1971), p. 1618

KENNEDY, M. Sleeve note for ASD 2672

CORONATION ODE (Op. 44)

ACHENBACH, A. 'Coronation Ode', *Gramophone* 71 (June 1993), p. 83

ANON. 'The Sheffield Musical Festival', *Musical Times* 43 (November 1902), p. 730

HARVEY, T. 'Coronation Ode', *Gramophone* 54 (May 1977), pp. 1718+23

KENNEDY, M. 'Coronation Ode', *Gramophone* 65 (May 1988), p. 1630

KENNEDY, M. Sleeve note for CMS7 64209–2 (1993)

KENNEDY, M. Sleeve note for RL 25074 (1977)

SMITH, H.W. 'Letters to the editor: Elgar's Coronation Ode', *Musical Times* 44 (February 1903), p. 115

THE CROWN OF INDIA (Op. 66)

ANON. 'Masque at the Coliseum', *Musical Times* 53 (April 1912), p. 257

THE CROWN OF INDIA SUITE (Op. 66)

HARVEY, T. 'Crown of India Suite', *Gramophone* 48 (April 1971), p. 1618

KENNEDY, M. Sleeve note for ASD 2672 (1971)

KENNEDY, M. Sleeve note for CDM7 63280–2 (1990)

SANDERS, A. 'Elgar:Orchestral Works', *Gramophone* 67 (March 1990), p. 1603

SCOWCROFT, p. L. 'The Crown of India March: a new re-orchestration', *Elgar Society Journal* 6 (May 1990), p. 7

LE DRAPEAU BELGE (Op. 79)

COLLETT, B. Sleeve note for SHE CD 9602 (1988)
MOORE, J.N. 'Le drapeau Belge', *Gramophone* 52 (February 1975), p. 1491
SANDERS, A. 'Le drapeau Belge', *Gramophone* 65 (May 1988), p. 1628

THE DREAM OF GERONTIUS (Op. 38)

ANDERSON, R. 'Worcester', *Musical Times* 125 (April 1984), p. 224
ANDERSON, W.R. 'More school certificate works: Elgar's Dream, reality and aftermath', *Music Teacher* 29 (August 1950), pp. 345+
ANON. 'Barbirolli conducts Dream of Gerontius', *Musical America* 79 (February 1959), p. 265
ANON. 'The Birmingham Music Festival' *Musical Times* 41 (November 1900), pp. 731–32
ANON. 'Classical recordings', *Fanfare* 3 (no.5) 1980, pp. 74–76
ANON. 'The Dream of Gerontius', *Musical Times* 41 (November 1900), pp. 731–32
ANON. 'The Dream of Gerontius in Düsseldorf', *Musical Times* 43 (February 1902), pp. 114–15
ANON. 'Elgar's Dream of Gerontius in Germany', *Musical Times* 43 (January 1902), p. 34
ANON. 'The first performance of The Dream of Gerontius in Paris', *Musical Times* 47 (June 1906), p. 402
ANON. 'The German press on Dr.Elgar's Dream of Gerontius', *Musical Times* 43 (February 1902), p. 100
ANON. 'Occasional Notes', *Musical Times* 41 (October 1900), p. 654
ANON. 'Occasional Notes', *Musical Times* 42 (June 1901), p. 388
ANON. 'Occasional Notes – review of the Düsseldorf performance', *Musical Times* 42 (December 1901), p. 805
ANON. 'Preview of the first performance in Paris', *Musical Times* 47 (May 1906), p. 321
ANON. 'Review of the Vienna performance', *Musical Times* 46 (December 1905), p. 802
ANON.'Sir Edward's Dream', *Time* 73, 2 February 1959, p. 46
ASHMAN, M. 'Elgar's Dream: Sir Adrian Boult talks to Mike Ashman', *Records and Recordings* 19 (April 1976), p. 20
BARBIROLLI, J./ROBERTSON, A. Sleeve note for ALP2101-2 (1965)
BAUGHAN, E.A. [The Dream of Gerontius], *Musical Standard* 13 October 1900, pp. 91–96
BENNETT, W. 'A Memory from the Choir', *Monthly Musical Record* 63 (February 1933), pp. 96–99
BLYTH, A. 'The Dream of Gerontius', *Gramophone* 52 (April 1975), pp. 1844+1849
BLYTH, A. 'The Dream of Gerontius', *Gramophone* 67 (December 1989), pp. 1183–84

BLYTH, A. 'The Dream of Gerontius', *Gramophone* 68 (June 1990), pp. 94+97

BROWN, p. 'Music in concert', *Choir* 54 (June 1963), pp. 100–102

BURY, D. 'Ludwig Wüllner and the Westminster Gerontius', *Elgar Society Journal* 2 (June 1981), pp. 9–13

CRANKSHAW, G. 'Sir Adrian's first complete recording of Gerontius', *Records and Recordings* 19 (April 1976), p. 21

CRICHTON, R. 'Choral', *Musical Times* 113 (August 1972), p. 383

DANN, M.G. 'The harmonic techniques of Edward Elgar based on the Dream of Gerontius', Mus.M. thesis, Eastman School of Music, University of Rochester (New York), 1937

DAY, E. 'Interpreting Gerontius: personal memories of Elgar in rehearsal', *Musical Times* 110 (June 1969), pp. 607–8

ERICSON, R. 'Reward for patience: Gerontius dreams on vinyl', *High Fidelity* 6 (January 1956), p. 112

EVES, G. 'Correspondence: Heddle Nash', *Gramophone* 49 (August 1971), p. 380

FENTON, J. 'Elgar's use of the leitmotif in The Dream of Gerontius', *Music Teacher* 54 (January 1975), pp. 11–12; (February 1975), pp. 12–13

GORTON, C.V. 'The Dream of Gerontius: an Interpretation of the Libretto', London, Novello, 1906

GREENHAIGH, M. 'Records: Gerontius', *Music and Musicians* 25 (October 1976), p. 41

HOLD, T. 'Letters to the Editor: Elgar's interpretations', *Musical Times* 110 (October 1969), p. 1039

HURD, M. 'Elgar: The Dream of Gerontius', *Music in Education* 39 (no.374) 1975, pp. 165–66

JACOBSON, B. 'Edward Elgar', *Stereo Review* 30 (May 1973), p. 112

JAEGER, A.J. 'The Dream of Gerontius: Book of Words with Analytical and Descriptive Notes' London, Novello, 1901

JAEGER, A.J. 'Mr.Elgar's setting of The Dream of Gerontius', *Musical Times* 41 (October 1900), pp. 663–64+73 (Reprinted from the Birmingham Festival Programme Book)

KENNEDY, M. 'Gerontius after 75 years', *Daily Telegraph*, 4 October 1975, p. 9

KENNEDY, M., etc. Sleeve note for CHS7 63376–2 (1990)

KENNEDY, M., etc. Sleeve note for CMS7 63185–2 (1989)

LESSMANN, O. [Comments on The Dream of Gerontius, originally appearing in *Allegemeine Musik Zeitung*], *Musical Times* 42 (January 1901), p. 20

LEWIS, G.H. 'Richter and Gerontius: a Strange Case of Incomprehension', *Elgar Society Newsletter*, no.4 (new series), January 1978, pp. 16–19

MAXWELL, M. [The Dream of Gerontius], *American Record Guide* 32 (May 1966), pp. 796–97+

MOORE, J.N. and BLYTH, A. Sleeve note for Testament SBT 2025 (1993)

MOORES, I.G. 'Sir Edward Elgar and Cardinal John Henry Newman. The Dream of Gerontius: Intimacy without Contact', *Elgar Society Journal* 6 (January 1989), pp. 3–7

NETTEL, R. [The Dream of Gerontius] *in* 'Ordeal by Music' London, Oxford University Press, 1945

POWELL, D.M. 'The first performance of Gerontius', *Musical Times* 100 (February 1959), pp. 78–79

ROBERTSON, A. 'The Dream of Gerontius', *Gramophone* 32 (May 1955), p. 534

ROBERTSON, A. 'The Dream of Gerontius', *Gramophone* 43 (October 1965), pp. 206–7

ROBERTSON, A. Sleeve note for 33CX1247–48 (1955)

SIMMONS, D. 'London music', *Musical Opinion* 96 (June 1973), pp. 505–8

STEWART, A. 'Maximalist Elgar', *Gramophone* 71 (October 1993), pp. 26–27

WAITE, V. 'An angel as ever, God bless him: Elgar and Parry', *Elgar Society Newsletter* no.5 (new series), May 1978, pp. 5–9

YOUNG, P.M. 'Newman, Elgar and The Dream of Gerontius', *Elgar Society Journal* 6 (January 1990), pp. 4–12

DREAM CHILDREN (*Enfants d'un Rêve*, OP. 43)

MOORE, J.N. 'Dream Children', *Gramophone* 52 (February 1975), p. 1491

ELEGY FOR STRINGS (Op. 58)

HARVEY, T. 'Elegy', *Gramophone* 44 (December 1966), pp. 315–16

MOORE, J.N. 'Elegy', *Gramophone* 52 (February 1975), p. 1491

EXERCISE FOR THE THIRD FINGER

ELGAR, E.W. 'Elgar as Fiddler', *Daily Telegraph*, 24 December 1920, p. 4

FALSTAFF (Op. 68)

ANON. [Falstaff], *Philadelphia Orchestra Program Notes* 14 January 1965, pp. 13+

ANON. [Falstaff], *Pittsburgh Symphony Orchestra Program Notes* 29 March 1963, pp. 25–30

ANON. 'The Jubilee of Elgar's Falstaff', *Choir* 54 (December 1963), pp. 219–20

ANON. [Review of Elgar: Falstaff, 1933], *Musical Times* 73 (March 1933), p. 234

ANON. 'What is a Hoodoo?' *Musical Opinion* 78 (December 1954), pp. 133–34

ELGAR, E.W. 'Falstaff: an analytical essay by the composer', *Musical Times* 54 (September 1913), pp. 575–81 Published separately by Novello & Co., 1933

ELLIOTT, J.H. 'Letters to the editor: Elgar's Falstaff', *Musical Times* 70 (September 1929), p. 837

GARVIE, P. 'Falstaff and the King: reflections on Elgar', *Canadian Music Journal* 2 (Autumn 1957), pp. 30–32

GELATT, R. 'Elgar's memorable and magical Falstaff', *High Fidelity* 5 (April 1955), p. 55

GOODWIN, N. Sleeve note for CDM7 69185–2 (1988)

GRAY-FISK, C. 'Letters to the editor: Elgar's Falstaff', *Musical Times* 70 (September 1929), p. 837

KENT, C. 'Falstaff: Elgar's Symphonic Study' in 'Edward Elgar: Music and Literature' (ed. Raymond Monk) Aldershot, Scolar Press, 1993

LADERMAN, E. 'Two by the Pittsburgh', *HiFi/Musical America* 16 (February 1966), pp. 139+

LORENZ, R. 'An amateur's study of Elgar's Falstaff', *Musical Times* 73 (November 1932), pp. 989–993

McVEAGH, D. 'Elgar and Falstaff' in 'Elgar Studies' (ed. Raymond Monk) Aldershot, Scolar Press, 1990

PIRIE, P.J. 'A fat knight and his music', *High Fidelity* 13 (January 1963), pp. 46–47

POLLARD, A. 'Falstaff', *Gramophone* 32 (August 1954), p. 101

REID, C. 'Strains again: Falstaff', *The Spectator* 1 May 1964, p. 590

RUSSELL, T. 'The Falstaff enigma', *Philharmonic Post* 6 (January-February 1952), p. 15

SANDERS, A. 'Falstaff', *Gramophone* 66 (November 1988), p. 878

SCHOLES, P. 'Elgar's Falstaff re-considered', *Musical Times* 70 (August 1929), pp. 696–98

TOVEY, D.F. 'Falstaff' in 'Essays in Musical Analysis': Volume 4 – Illustrative Music London, Oxford University Press, 1935–39

WOOD, R.W. 'Falstaff', *Music and Letters* 14 (April 1933), pp. 117–123

FRINGES OF THE FLEET

COLLETT, B. Sleeve note for SHE CD 9602 (1988)

SANDERS, A. 'Fringes of the Fleet', *Gramophone* 65 (May 1988), p. 1628

FROISSART (Op. 19)

HARVEY, T. 'Froissart', *Gramophone* 44 (December 1966), pp. 315–16

FROM THE GREEK ANTHOLOGY (Op. 45)

ANON. [From the Greek Anthology], *Musical Times* 44 (December 1903), p. 801

GENERAL

ABRAHAM, G. 'Pomp and poetry: a look at Sir Edward Elgar across a century', *High Fidelity* 7 (June 1957), pp. 44–46+

AFFELDER, P. 'A guide to Elgar on records', *High Fidelity* 7 (June 1957), p. 46

ALDER, M.B. 'Memories of a Pupil' in 'An Elgar Companion' (ed. C.Redwood) Ashbourne, Sequoia, 1982

ALLDRITT, K. 'Elgar on the journey to Hanley': a novel, London, Deutsch, 1979

ALLISON, J. 'Edward Elgar: sacred music', Bridgend, Seren Books, 1994

ANDERSON, R. 'A Creative Life: recent Elgar literature', *Musical Times* 125 (August 1984), pp. 442–44

ANDERSON, R. 'Elgar' (Master Musicians Series) London, Dent, 1993

ANDERSON, R. 'Elgar in Manuscript' London, The British Library, 1990

ANDERSON, R. 'Elgar's musical style', *Musical Times* 134 (December 1993), pp. 689–90+92

ANDERSON, R. 'Gertrude Walker: an Elgarian friendship', *Musical Times* 125 (December 1984), pp. 698–700

ANDERSON, R. [Review of Collet, P. & C., 1981], *Musical Times* 122 (December 1981), p. 822

ANDERSON, R. [Review of De la Noy, 1983], *Musical Times* 124 (November 1983), p. 682

ANDERSON, R. [Review of Kennedy: Elgar orchestral music, 1970], *Musical Times* 111 (November 1970), p. 111

ANDERSON, R. [Review of Moore: Elgar and his publishers, 1987], *Musical Times* 129 (February 1988), pp. 79–80

ANDERSON, R. [Review of Moore: Elgar, the Windflower Letters and Weaver: The Thirteenth Enigma, 1989], *Musical Times* 130 (December 1989), pp. 747–78

ANDERSON, R. [Review of Mundy, 1980], *Musical Times* 122 (February 1981), p. 108

ANDERSON, R. [Review of Parrott, 1971], *Musical Times* 112 (September 1971), pp. 858–59

ANDERSON, R. [Review of Redwood, 1983], *Musical Times* 124 (July 1983), pp. 428–29

ANDERSON, W.R. 'Introduction to the music of Elgar' London, Dobson, 1949

ANDERSON, W.R. [Review of Powell: Memories of a Variation, 1937], *Musical Times* 78 (November 1937), p. 954

ANDERSON de NAVARRO, M. [Elgar] *in* 'A few more memories' London, Hutchinson, 1936

ANON. 'The cello music of Elgar, Delius and Holst', *Music and Musicians*, 32 (July 1984), pp. 10–11

ANON. [Conferment of a D.Mus. degree on Elgar at the University of Cambridge], *Musical Times* 41 (November 1900), p. 728

ANON. [Conferment of D.Mus.degree on Elgar at Yale University], *Musical Times* 46 (August 1905), p. 528

ANON. 'Dr.Edward Elgar', *The Sketch* 62 (7 October 1903), pp. 418–19

ANON. 'Editorial: Documenting Elgar', *Music and Letters* 53 (July 1972), pp. 239–241

ANON. 'Edward Elgar', *Gramophone* 60 (August 1982), pp. 217–18

ANON. 'Edward Elgar', *Musical Times* 41 (October 1900), pp. 641–48

ANON. [Election of Elgar to the Athenaeum Club], *Musical Times* 45 (May 1904), p. 304

ANON. 'Elgar after thirty years' *Choir* 55 (February 1964), pp. 23–24

ANON. 'Elgar at 75', *Musical Times* 74 (January 1933), p. 38

ANON. 'Elgar at Severn House – I', *The World*, 22 October 1912

ANON. 'The Elgar centenary', *Musical Opinion* 80 (June 1957), p. 517

ANON. 'The Elgar centenary', *Musical Times* 98 (June 1957), pp. 301–302

ANON. 'Elgar centenary', *Musical Times* 98 (August 1957), p. 439

ANON. 'The Elgar Festival', *Musical Times* 45 (April 1904), pp. 241–43

ANON. 'The Elgar Festival', *Musical Times* 90 (May 1949), p. 152; 90 (July 1949), p. 242

ANON. 'Elgar manuscripts', *Music and Musicians* 19 (January 1971), p. 10

ANON. 'Elgar manuscripts', *Performing Right* no.54 (November 1970), p. 20

ANON. 'Elgar memorial concerts', *Musical Times* 75 (April 1934), p. 364

ANON. 'Elgar's Broadwood Piano', *British Library Newsletter* no.183 (January 1994), p. [1]

ANON. 'Elgar's Life and Career', *Musical Times* 75 (April 1934), pp. 314–18

ANON. 'The exhibition at Elgar's birthplace', *Musical Times* 76 (October 1935), p. 938

ANON. 'First comprehensive festival of the music of Elgar', *The Chesterian* 23 (April 1949), p. 107

ANON. 'Four piano pieces by Elgar, written in a Worcestershire lady's autograph book in the 1880s', *Musical Times* 123 (September 1982), p. 616

ANON. 'Gramophone notes' *Strad* 80 (January 1970), p. 437

ANON. 'Here and there', *Gramophone* 59 (July 1981), p. 142

ANON. 'High notes', *Musical Opinion* 112 (January 1989), p. 8

ANON. 'High notes', *Musical Opinion* 114 (December 1991), p. 439

ANON. 'Interview: Sir Edward Elgar backs a horse', *Daily Express* 19 December 1932. p. 11

ANON. [Knighthood for Elgar], *Musical Times* 45 (July 1904), p. 442

ANON. 'The late Lady Elgar' (obituary), *Musical Times* 60 (May 1920), p. 331

ANON. 'The Memorial Service in Worcester Cathedral', *Musical Times* 75 (April 1934), p. 313

ANON. 'Memorial window in Worcester Cathedral', *Musical Times* 76 (February 1935), p. 158

ANON. 'Musical Kipling', *Time* 69 (10 June 1957), p. 72

ANON. 'Notes and News – fading out of important works', *Musical Times* 83 (February 1942), p. 60

ANON. 'Notes and News – portrait of Elgar presented to Westminster School', *Musical Times* 84 (January 1943), p. 28

ANON. 'Notes and News – Walton's view of Elgar', *Musical Times* 84 (January 1943), p. 28

ANON. 'Notes of the day', *Monthly Musical Record* 85 (October 1955), pp. 197–200

ANON. 'Notes of the day', *Monthly Musical Record* 87 (July–August 1957), pp. 121–22

ANON. 'Occasional notes: appointment as Master of the King's Musick', *Musical Times* 65 (June 1924), p. 513

ANON. 'Occasional notes: bestowal of the O.M. on Elgar', *Musical Times* 52 (July 1911), p. 454

ANON. 'Occasional notes: conferment of the K.C.V.O. on Elgar', *Musical Times* 69 (February 1928), p. 139

ANON. 'Occasional notes: the Elgar manifesto', *Musical Times* 72 (June 1932), pp. 512–13

ANON. 'Occasional notes: Elgar's views on municipal subsidy of orchestras and concert halls', *Musical Times* 51 (January 1910), p. 18

ANON. 'Occasional notes: protest against Professor Dent's alleged injustice', *Musical Times* 72 (April 1931), pp. 326–28

ANON. £100,000 public appeal to save Elgar's birthplace', *Music Teacher* 55 (August 1976), p. 20

ANON. 'Opus record reviews: Elgar – Songs', *Musical America* 109, no.2 (1989), p. 61

ANON. 'Original Elgar manuscripts recovered', *Music Teacher* 50 (August 1971), p. 10

ANON. 'Portrait [Elgar] by Rothenstein', *Music and Letters* 1 (January 1920), p. 7

ANON. 'A portrait of Elgar', *Musical Times* 92 (March 1951), pp. 124–125

ANON. 'A question of honour', *Delius* no.107 (Summer/Autumn 1991), pp. 32–34

ANON. 'Record notes: Images of Elgar, 5LPs', *World* 2 (27 February 1973), p. 57

ANON. 'Recordings in review', *Musical America* 109 (1989), pp. 54–56

ANON. 'Reflections of yesterday', *Canon* 10 (June 1957), pp. 370–371

ANON. [Review of Buckley, 1904], *Musical Times* 45 (October 1904), p. 652

ANON. [Review of Maine, 1933], *Musical Times* 73 (July 1933), p. 608

ANON. [Review of Newman: Elgar, 1906], *Musical Times* 47 (July 1906), pp. 472+481

ANON. [Review of Sheldon, 1932], *Musical Times* 75 (May 1934), p. 418

ANON. 'Self-taught Genius – Life Stories of Endeavour. No.XLVII: Sir Edward Elgar', *Ideas*, 8 November 1911, pp. 6–7

ANON. 'Sir Edward Elgar 1857–1934', *London Music* 12 (1957), p. 9

ANON. 'Some of Elgar's friends', *Musical Times* 75 (April 1934), pp. 319–320

ANON. 'Two promising young men: Elgar and Delius', *Music Teacher* 29 (December 1950), p. 583 (reprinted from *The Gazette* 1899)

ANON. 'X lived here', *Music and Musicians* 11 (November 1962), pp. 46–47

ANON. 'Wanted £25,000 for Elgar lovers' *Musical Opinion* 90 (July 1967), pp. 562–63

ANON. 'Wanted £25,000 for Elgar lovers', *Music Teacher* 46 (July 1967), p. 19

ASHLEN, C.G. 'Grammofonens veteraner: Sir Edward Elgar, Bart., O.M., K.C.V.O. (1857–1934)', *Music Review* 28 (no.6) 1973, pp. 399–402

ATKINS, E.W. '1890 – The Birth of a Friendship', Worcester Three Choirs Festival Programme Book, 1990

ATKINS, E.W. '1890–1990. The Centenary of the Birth of a Friendship: Edward Elgar–Ivor Atkins. Elgar and Atkins and their influence on Three Choirs Festivals' Woldingham, E.W. Atkins, 1990

ATKINS, E.W. 'The Elgar–Atkins Friendship', Newton Abbot, David and Charles, 1984

ATKINS, E.W. 'George Robertson Sinclair', Hereford Three Choirs Festival Programme Book, 1991

ATKINS, E.W. 'Music in the Provinces: the Elgar–Atkins Letters', *Proceedings of the Royal Musical Association* 84 (1957–58), pp. 27–42

ATKINS, E.W. 'S.T.P. ' [Letter to the Editor], *Musical Times* 125 (June 1984), p. 313

[ATWATER, F.V.] 'Mr.Edward Elgar and his works', *Musical Courier*, October 1896

BAIRSTOW, E.C. 'Elgar's Songs', *Music Student* 8 (August 1916), pp. 349–350

BAKER, J. 'Letters to the editor: Elgar and Mozart's G minor symphony', *Musical Times* 76 (December 1935), pp. 1123–24

BALDWYN, R. 'Elgar experience', *Royal College of Music Magazine* 80 (no.3) 1984, p. 129

BANFIELD, S. [Elgar's Songs] *in* 'Sensibility and English Song' (2 volumes) Cambridge, Cambridge University Press, 1985

BANFIELD, S. [Review of Alldritt, 1979] Musical Times 120 (October 1979), p. 830

BANFIELD, S. [Review of Redwood, 1982], *Music and Letters* 66 (April 1985), pp. 169–170

BANFIELD, S. [Review of Young: Alice Elgar, 1978], *Music and Letters* 60 (April 1979), pp. 227–78

BARBIROLLI, J. 'Forty Years with Elgar's Music' *in* 'Edward Elgar: Centenary Sketches' (ed. H.A.Chambers) London, Novello, 1957

BARTELS, B. 'The English symphony in the 19th century', M.A. thesis, University of Nebraska, 1967

BAYLISS, S. 'Elgar in his letters', *Music and Letters* 38 (April 1957), pp. 124–28

BAYLISS, S. [Review of Young: Elgar, O.M., 1955] *Music and Letters* 37 (January 1956), pp. 73–75

BICKERTON-JONES, W.H. 'To Sir Edward Elgar, O.M.,K.C.V.O. (M.K.M) Born 2 June 1857 – a poem', *Musical Times* 71 (June 1930), p. 497

BLACKING, J. 'Can musical universals be heard?' *World Music* 19 (nos.1–2) 1977, pp. 14–18

BLAKE, C.E. 'A Family Retrospect' *in* 'Edward Elgar: Centenary Sketches' (ed. H.A. Chambers) London, Novello, 1957

BLAKE, C.E. 'My Memories of my Father', *Music and Musicians* 10 (June 1957), p. 11

BLAKE, C.E. 'Re-opening of the Elgar birthplace', *Music* (S.M.A.) 2 no.1 (1967), pp. 46–47

BLAKE, C.E. and others [Letters to the Editor], *Musical Times* 110 (January 1969), p. 322

BLISS, A. [Elgar] *in* 'As I Remember' London, Faber, 1970

BLISS, A. 'Edward Elgar', *Elgar Society Journal* 1 (September 1979), pp. 7–9 (Reprint of article in *Berrow's Worcester Journal*, 7 June 1957 p. 5) Also reprinted in G. ROSCOW 'Bliss on Music', OUP, 1991

BLOM, E.[Review of Powell:Memories of a Variation, 2nd. ed. 1947], *Music and Letters* 29 (January 1948), pp. 85–86

BODEN, A. [Elgar] in 'Three Choirs: a history of the Festival' Stroud, Sutton, 1992

BOLITHO, H. [Elgar] in 'Older People' London, Cobden-Sanderson, 1935

BOOSEY, L.A. 'Some thoughts about Elgar', Tempo no. 39 (Spring 1956), pp. 28–30

BORROWDALE, J.H. 'Letters: More Elgar and Rosa', Music and Musicians 22 (May 1974), p. 4+

BOULT, A. 'Composer as Conductor' in 'Edward Elgar: Centenary Sketches' (ed. H.A. Chambers) London, Novello, 1957

BOULT, A. [Elgar] in 'My Own Trumpet' London, Hamilton, 1973

BOULT, A. 'Elgar as a conductor', Recorded Sound no. 48 (October 1972), pp. 112–115

BRENT-SMITH, A.E. 'The Humour of Elgar', Music and Letters 16 (January 1935), pp. 20–25

BRETT, E. 'Letters to the editor: Elgar and the public', Musical Times 72 (February 1931), p. 155

BUCKLEY, R.J. 'Sir Edward Elgar' London, J.Lane/Bodley Head, 1904

BURGE, T.A. 'Edward Elgar', The Ampleforth Journal, July 1902, pp. 26–27

BURLEY, R. and CARRUTHERS, F.C. 'Edward Elgar: The Record of a Friendship', London, Barrie and Jenkins, 1972

BURNS, R.C. [Elgar conducts Elgar], A.R.S.C. 7 no.1–2 (1975), pp. 105–120

BURY, D. 'Elgar, A.C.Benson and 1914', Elgar Society Journal 4 (January 1985), pp. 9–13

BURY, D. 'Elgar and James Whewell – A study of the North Staffordshire Choral Society', Elgar Society Journal 2 (September 1981), pp. 10–16

BURY, D. 'Elgar and the Two Mezzos' London, Thames, 1984

BUSH, G. 'Elgar's Songs' in 'The Romantic Age 1800–1914' (ed. N.Temperley) London, Athlone Press, 1981

BUTTREY, J. 'Correspondence: Elgar and Lady Mary Lygon', Music and Letters 54 (July 1973), pp. 382–83

BUTTREY, J. 'Edward J.Dent and Elgar', Elgar Society Newsletter no.3 (new series), September 1977, pp. 8 – 10

BUTTREY, J. 'Elgar and Lady Mary Lygon', Music and Letters 54 (January 1973), pp. 122–123; (July 1973), pp. 382–383

CAIRNS, D. 'The master touch', The Sunday Times, 17 August 1975, p. 23

CAPEL, R. and McNAUGHT, W. 'The Elgar Festival', Musical Times 90 (July 1949), p. 242

CARDUS, N. 'Elgar' in 'A Composer's Eleven' London, Cape, 1958

CARDUS, N. 'Elgar and Mahler', Radio Times, 1 May 1931 Reprinted as 'Elgar and Mahler: more the Nationalists', Elgar Society Journal 6 (May 1989), pp. 4–6

CAREY, H. [Elgar] in 'Duet for two voices: an informal biography of E.J.Dent' Cambridge, Cambridge University Press, 1979

CHAMBERS, H.A. 'Edward Elgar: Centenary Sketches' London, Novello, 1957

CHAMBERS, H.A. 'Elgar at Croydon', Musical Times 95 (July 1954), p. 384

CHAMBERS, H.A. 'Publishing Office Memories' in 'Edward Elgar: Centenary Sketches' (ed. H.A.Chambers) London, Novello, 1957

CHAPMAN, C.E. 'Text setting in the part-songs of Edward Elgar' D.M.A. thesis, University of Illinois, 1988

CHAPMAN, E. 'The Macnaghten Concerts', *Composer* no.57 (Spring 1976), pp. 13–18

CLARK, D. 'My Dear Charles . . . Elgar – Man of Letters' *Elgar Society Journal* 5 (May 1987), pp. 9–16

COBBETT, W.W. 'Elgar's shorter violin works', *Music Student* 8 (August 1916), p. cccxlii

COCKSHOOT, J.V. [Review of Parrott, 1971], *Music and Letters* 52 (October 1971), pp. 435–36

COHEN, H. [Elgar] *in* 'A Bundle of Time' London, Faber, 1969

COLBECH, D. 'Elgar – The Astrological Connection', *Elgar Society Journal* 6 (January 1989), pp. 12–13 + 16 ; (May 1989), pp. 8–9

COLLES, H.C. 'Edward Elgar' *in* 'Grove's Dictionary of Music and Musicians', 4th edition (editor: H.C.Colles), London, Macmillan, 1940 Volume 2, pp. 149–157 Supplementary volume (1945), pp. 191–206

COLLES, H.C. 'Edward Elgar' *in* 'Grove's Dictionary of Music and Musicians', 5th edition (editor: E.Blom), London, Macmillan, 1954 Volume 2, pp. 909–928 Supplementary volume (1961), p. 121

COLLETT, B. 'Elgar Country' London, Thames, 1981

COLLETT, P. 'Elgar lived here' London, Thames, 1981

COLLETT, P. 'An Elgar Travelogue' London, Thames, 1983

CONNOLLY, J. 'Edward Elgar: fantasies and realities', *Composer* no.28 (Summer 1968), pp. 3–6

CONQUEST, R. 'New variations on Elgar', *Spectator*, 19 December 1970, p. 801

CONRAT, H. 'Edward Elgar', *Neue Musik-Zeitung* 3 (24 December 1903), pp. 33–34

COOKE, A. 'Letters: Elgar and Stanford', *Music and Musicians* 21 (June 1973), p. 5

COOPER, B. AND BROWNE, T. Letters to the Editor: Elgar's Enigmas', *Musical Times* 111 (August 1970), p. 801

CORDOVA, R.de 'Illustrated Interviews: Dr.Elgar', *Strand Magazine* 27 (May 1904), pp. 537–544

CREDITOR, B. 'Quintessence', *Clarinet* 15 no.2 (1988), p. 11

CRICHTON, R. 'Elgar and the Theatre', *Financial Times* 30 December 1968, p. 3

CRUFT, A. 'The Elgar dedication', *Composer* no.44 (Summer 1972), p. 13

CRUFT, A. 'The Elgar dedication', *Royal College of Music Magazine* 68 no.3 (1972), pp. 81–82

CUMBERLAND, G. 'A day with Sir Edward Elgar', *Musical World* (15 January 1906), pp. 8–9

CUMBERLAND, G. 'Elgar at Plâs Gwyn', *Musical World* (15 January 1906)

CUMBERLAND, G. [Edward Elgar] *in* 'Set Down in Malice' London, Richards, 1919

CUMBERLAND, G. 'First Impressions: no.1 – Sir Edward Elgar', *Musical World* (16 December 1905), pp. 243–4

CURTIS, G.R.K. 'Elgar's Symphonies – a light in the darkness', *Records and Recordings* 26 (January 1982), pp. 10–11

DALY, F. 'The triple tragedy', *Musical Opinion* 107 (August 1984), pp. 339–340

DANN, M.G. 'Elgar's use of the sequence', *Music and Letters* 19 (July 1938), pp. 255–264

DAWES, F. 'Elgar's cottage in Sussex', *Musical Times* 112 (November 1971), pp. 1069–70

DEAN, W. [Review of Anderson: Introduction to the music of Elgar], *Music and Letters* 31 (October 1950), pp. 357–359

DEAN, W. [Review of McVeagh: Edward Elgar – his life and music,1955], *Music and Letters* 37 (January 1956), pp. 71–73

DE LA NOY, M. 'Elgar the Man' London, Allen Lane, 1983

DELONG, K. 'Recent Victoriana' *J.A.L.S.* 24 (1988), pp. 74–85

DENNISON, P. 'Elgar and Wagner', *Music and Letters* 66 (April 1985), pp. 93–107

DENNISON, P. 'Elgar's Musical Apprenticeship' *in* 'Elgar Studies' (ed. Raymond Monk) Aldershot, Scolar Press, 1990

DIBBLE, J.C. [Elgar] *in* 'C.Hubert H.Parry – his life and music' Oxford, Oxford University Press, 1992

DIBBLE, J.C. 'Elgar and Parry: a new perspective', *Musical Times* 125 (November 1984), pp. 639–643

DICKINSON, A.E. 'The drama behind Elgar's music', *Music and Letters* 23 (April 1942), pp. 116–125

DICKINSON, A.E. 'The isolation of Elgar', *Music Survey* 3 (June 1951), pp. 233–40

DOMVILLE,E. 'Music for King and Country', *Fugue* 3 (June 1979), pp. 20–24+

DREW, D. 'London', *Musical Courier* 156 (July 1957), p. 17

DUCKENFIELD, B. [Elgar] *in* 'O Lovely Knight: a biography of Sir Landon Ronald' London, Thames, 1991

DUNHILL, T. 'Sir Edward Elgar' London, Blackie, 1938

DYER, L. 'Music by British Composers – a series of complete catalogues: no. 2 – Sir Edward Elgar' London, Oxford University Press, 1931

EDWARDS, F.G. 'Edward Elgar', *Musical Times* 41 (October 1900), pp. 641–648

EDWARDS, N. 'The lady behind the shower', *Elgar Society Journal* 3 (January 1984), pp. 10–11

EICKHOFF, L. 'Burglary!' *Elgar Society Journal* 5 (January 1988), pp. 11–14

EICKHOFF, L. 'The Elgars at Hampstead', *Elgar Society Journal* 1 (May 1980), pp. 13–15

EICKHOFF, L. 'Further notes on Severn House', *Elgar Society Journal* 3 (September 1984), pp. 7–9

ELGAR, E.W. 'Brahms's chamber music', *Malvern Gazette* 21 December 1886; 29 January 1887

ELGAR, E.W. 'A Christmas Fable' [God made a puppy] Elgar's Christmas card for 1932

ELGAR, E.W. *Foreword* to 'Forgotten Worcester' by H.A. Leicester Worcester, Bayliss, 1930

ELGAR, E.W. 'A Frisk', *Times Literary Supplement*,6 August 1925, p. 521

ELGAR, E.W. 'Gray,Walpole,West and Ashton, the Quadruple Alliance', *Times Literary Supplement*, 4 September 1919, p. 473

ELGAR, E.W. 'H.M.V.', *Recorded Sound* 2 (January 1963), p. iv

ELGAR, E.W. [Letter about Hubert Parry], *Music and Letters* 1 (January 1920), p. 165

ELGAR, E.W. 'Musical Notation', *Musical Times* 61 (August 1920), pp. 513–15

ELGAR, E.W. 'My visit to Delius', *Daily Telegraph*, 1 July 1933, p. 5

ELGAR, E.W. 'A poet as critic', *Daily Telegraph* 12 April 1919, p. 4

ELGAR, E.W. 'Poluphloisboisterous', *Times Literary Supplement* 2 August 1923, p. 520

ELGAR, E.W. *Preface* to 'The Singing of the Future' by David Ffrangcon-Davies, London, John Lane, 1902

ELGAR, E.W. *Preface* to 'System in Musical Notation' by H.E. Button, London, Novello, 1920

ELGAR, E.W. Programme notes for the Worcestershire Philharmonic Society, 1898–1903

ELGAR, E.W. 'Scott and Shakespeare', *Times Literary Supplement* 21 July 1921, p. 468

ELGAR, E.W. 'Swift in Bury Street,' *Times Literary Supplement* 10 August 1922, p. 521

ELGAR, E.W. 'The vernal anemones: a beautiful native', *The Times* 28 April 1924

EVANS, E., etc. 'Three critics on Elgar', *Musical Times* 75 (April 1934), p. 323

EVANS, R.J. 'Orchestral performance practice in the nineteenth century with specific reference to Elgar', M.Phil. thesis, New College, Oxford, in preparation

FANSELAU, R. 'Die Orgel im Werk Edward Elgars', Gottingen, Funke-Kassel, Baerenreiter, 1974

FENBY, E. 'Eric Fenby on Elgar', *Delius* no.59 (April 1978), pp. 13–14

FENEMORE-JONES, T. 'The Clock Chimes of Eaton Socon', *Elgar Society Journal* 7 (May 1991), pp. 14–20

FIFIELD, C. [Elgar] *in* 'True Artist and true Friend: a biography of Hans Richter', Oxford, Oxford University Press, 1993

FOREMAN, L. [Elgar] *in* 'From Parry to Britten: British Music in Letters 1900–1945', London, Batsford, 1987

FOREMAN, L. 'The revival of Elgar's choral music', *Musical Opinion* 98 (February 1975), pp. 239–240+

FORREST, D.M. [Review: Reed, 1939], *Music and Letters* 20 (July 1939), pp. 320–21

FOSS, H.J. 'Elgar and his Age', *Music and Letters* 16 (January 1935), pp. 5–12

FOX-STRANGWAYS, A.H. 'Elgar: an obituary', *Music and Letters* 15 (April 1934), pp. 109–111

FOX-STRANGWAYS, A.H [Obituary of Alice Elgar], *The Times*, 8 April 1920, p. 12

GAISBERG, F.W. 'Elgarian' *in* 'Music on Record', New York, Robert Hale, 1949

GARVIE, P. 'Falstaff and the King: reflections on Elgar', *Canadian Music Journal* 2 (Autumn 1957), pp. 26–32

GATENS, W.J. [Review: Music for organ, edited by R. Anderson and C. Kent], *Music and Letters* 70 (August 1989), pp. 444–46

GENTLE, L.I. 'Letters to the editor: An Elgar hymn' *Musical Times* 120 (October 1979), p. 813

GLINES, D. 'Three prose tone poems', *Music News* 4 no.2 (1974), p. 17

GODDARD, S. 'Contemporary British music', *Canon* 12 (February 1959), pp. 226–27

GODMAN, S. 'The Elgars of Dover,' *Musical Times* 90 (July 1949), pp. 245–46

GODMAN, S. 'Letters to the editor: The Elgars of Dover', *Musical Times* 89 (January 1948), p. 27

GOOSSENS, E. [Elgar] *in* 'Overture and Beginners', London, Methuen, 1951

GOSDEN, O. 'The Fittons', *Elgar Society Journal* 2 (January 1982), pp. 11–13

GRACE, H. [Review of Dunhill, 1938], *Musical Times* 80 (March 1939), pp. 187–88

GRACE, H. [Review of Reed: Elgar, 1939], *Musical Times* 80 (June 1939), pp. 437–38

GRACE, H. [Review of Reed: Elgar as I knew him, 1936], *Musical Times* 77 (November 1936), pp. 998–99

GRACE, H. [Review of Shera,1931], *Musical Times* 74 (August 1933), pp. 708–9

GRACE, H./McNAUGHT, W. 'Edward Elgar: 2 June 1857–23 February 1934', *Musical Times* 75 (April 1934), pp. 305–13

GRAFTON, M. 'Family opposed to Elgar project', *Daily Telegraph* 27 August 1994, p. 14

GRAVES, D. 'Discord over memorial to Elgar', *Daily Telegraph* 20 August 1994, p. 10

GRAY, C. [Edward Elgar] *in* 'A Survey of Contemporary Music', London, Oxford University Press, 1924

GRAY, M. 'A man and his music', *Strad* 68 (May 1957), pp. 16+

GREENE, H.P. [Elgar] *in* 'Charles Villiers Stanford', London, Arnold, 1935

GREENFIELD, E. 'Elgar: the man and his music', *S.A. Music Teacher* no.107 (1985), pp. 14–15

GREENFIELD, E. 'Eureka! Auld enigmas be forgot', *Guardian* 28 February 1970

GRIFFITHS, A.C. 'The 78 Era' (Volume 3: The Elgar Edition – The Complete Electronic Recordings of Sir Edward Elgar), London, E.M.I., 1993

GROGAN, C. 'Elgar, Streatfeild and The Pilgrim's Progress' *in* 'Edward Elgar: Music and Literature' (ed. Raymond Monk), Aldershot, Scolar Press, 1993

GROGAN, C. [Review of Anderson: Elgar in manuscript, 1990], *Music and Letters* 73 (February 1992), pp. 136–39

GROGAN, C. [Review of Anderson: Elgar in manuscript, 1990], *Musical Times* 133 (February 1992), p. 80

GROGAN, C. [Review of Monk: Elgar Studies, 1990], *Musical Times* 132 (April 1991), p. 197

GUNSTON, D. 'Edward Elgar: the man behind the music', *Contemporary Review* 235 (October 1979), pp. 206–209 + 261

GUNSTON, D. 'Edward Elgar: the man behind the music', *Musical Opinion* 101 (March 1978), pp. 247–48

GUYVER, D. 'Edward Elgar and Edward German. Friendship and Correspondence', *Elgar Society Journal* 4 (May 1985), pp. 15–18; (September 1985), pp. 10–17

HADOW, W.H. [Elgar] *in* 'Collected Essays', London, Oxford University Press,1928

HALE, A.M. 'Letters to the editor: The Elgar protest', *Musical Times* 72 (April 1931), p. 350

HALL, R.A. 'Elgar and the intonation of British English', *Gramophone* 31 (June 1953), pp. 6–7

HALLET, R. 'Following a composer on wheels. Elgar and the Malvern Hills', *Country Life* 168 (30 October 1980), pp. 1590–92

HAMILTON, G. 'Elgar and the Baker family', *Musical Times* 120 (February 1979), pp. 121–22

HAMILTON-PATERSON, J. 'Gerontius': a novel, London, Vintage, 1989

HARRIS, R. 'Elgar Festival', *Music and Musicians* 28 (August 1980), p. 61; 29 (September 1980), p. 54

HARRISON, J. 'Elgar, Master of the Orchestra', Worcester, Elgar Society, 1957

HARRISON, J. 'Letters of Edward Elgar', *Musical Times* 98 (January 1957), pp. 20–21

HARVEY, T. 'A society has been formed . . .' *Gramophone* 40 (February 1963), pp. 380–81

HASSELT, L.van 'Elgar op bezoek', *Men en Melodie* 32 (February 1977), pp. 46–51

HELM, E. 'The Elgar case', *Music Review* 18 (May 1957), pp. 101–105

HERRMANN, B. 'An American Voice' *in* 'Edward Elgar Centenary Sketches' (ed. H.A.Chambers), London, Novello, 1957

HESSE, L.W. 'Elgar, Delius and Holst', *Musica* 38 no.4 (1984), pp. 341–44

HILL, R. 'Elgar', *Disc* 3 (Autumn 1949), pp. 147–49

HILL, R. 'When Elgar played for £2/12/6d', *Radio Times*, 19 November 1937, p. 15

HODGKINS, G. 'Elgar in North London', *Elgar Society Journal* 2 (May 1981), pp. 13–15; (September 1981), pp. 16–19

HODGKINS, G. 'Elgar's music for Powick Asylum', *Elgar Society Journal* 6 (January 1989), pp. 17–18

HODGKINS, G. 'Elgar's visit to Llangranog', *Elgar Society Newsletter* no.6 (May 1975), pp. 10–15

HODGKINS, G. 'Providence and Art. A study in Elgar's religious beliefs', London, The Elgar Society, 1979

HODGKINS, G. 'A sort of Anglican Eisteddfod. Elgar and the Madresfield Music Competition', *Elgar Society Journal* 6 (January 1989), pp. 8–11

HOLLANDER, H. 'Elgar in der Gegenwart', *Neue Zeitschrift fur Musik* 120 (November 1959), pp. 552–54

HOMFREY, T. 'Philharmonia Elgar cycle', *Music and Musicians* 27 (April 1979), pp. 57–58

HORTON, J. 'Two possible Elgarian allusions', *Musical Times* 101 (August 1960), pp. 490–92

HOWES, F.S. 'Elgar (1857–1934)' *in* 'The Heritage of Music', volume 3, edited by H.J. Foss, London, Oxford University Press, 1951

HOWES, F. [Elgar] in 'The English Musical Renaissance', London, Secker and Warburg, 1966

HOWES, F.S. 'Nimrod on Strauss', *Musical Times* 111 (June 1970), pp. 590–91

HOWES, F.S. 'The Two Elgars', *Music and Letters* 16 (January 1935), pp. 26–29

HUGHES, M. 'The Duc d'Elgar: Making a Composer Gentleman' in 'Music and the Politics of Culture' (ed. C.Norris), London, Lawrence and Wishart, 1989

HULL,Lady (ed. J.O'Callaghan) 'A Memoir of Elgar', *Elgar Society Journal* 7 (January 1991), pp. 11–13 (Part 1); (May 1991), pp. 9–14 (Part 2)

HULL, P. 'Elgar at Hereford,' *Royal Academy of Music Magazine* (1960), p. 6+

HULL, P. 'Some personal memories of Elgar', *Making Music* no.34 (Summer 1957), pp. 5–7. Reprinted in *Elgar Society Journal* 3 (May 1984), pp. 7–9

HULL, R. 'Three British composers: Elgar, Delius and Holst', *Musical Times* 100 (July 1959), pp. 380–2

HUNT, R. 'Elgar and the common touch', *Musical Opinion* 68 (April 1945), pp. 200–201

HURD, M. 'Elgar,' London, Faber, 1969

HURD, M. 'The Novello Archives', *Musical Times* 127 (December 1986), pp. 687–88

HUSSEY, W. 'Emotionalism in the music of Elgar', *Musical Times* 72 (March 1931), pp. 211–12

HUSSEY, D. 'The musician's gramophone', *Musical Times* 98 (August 1957), pp. 429–30

HUTCHINGS, A. 'The meditative English mind', *The Listener* 61 (23 April 1959), p. 736

HUTCHINSON, M. 'Elgar: the man and his map,' *Country Life* 13 August 1992, p. 76

INGLIS, A. 'Perspectives of Elgar', *Gramophone* 66 (February 1989), p. 1266

JACOBS, A. 'Elgar's solo songs,' *Musical Times* 90 (August 1949), pp. 267–68

JACOBSON, B. 'Making a case for Elgar', *Stereo Review* 38 (April 1977), pp. 76–80

JAEGER, A.J. 'Elgar's new choral works', *Musical Times* 49 (July 1908), pp. 453–54

JAEGER, A.J. 'Sir Edward Elgar's new part songs', *Elgar Society Journal* 6 (September 1989), pp. 19–23

JOHNSTONE, A. [Edward Elgar] in 'Musical Criticisms', Manchester, Manchester University Press, 1905

JONES, A.C. 'An Elgar curiosity', *Classical Guitar* 9 (November 1990), pp. 14–16

JONES, B. 'Wood Magic', *Strad* 95 (July 1984), pp. 188–90

JONES, T.F. 'Keeping the record straight', *Elgar Society Newsletter* no.1 (September 1973), pp. 16–19

JOSE, E. 'The significance of Elgar,' London, Heath Cranton, 1934

JUNGE, E. [Elgar] in 'Anthony Bernard – a life in music', Tunbridge Wells, Spellmount, 1992

KEETON, A.A. 'Elgar and Quotations', *Musical Opinion* 66 (August 1942), p. 373

KEHOE, J. 'Documentary Elgar', *Gramophone* 49 (December 1971), p. 1141

KELLER, H. 'Elgar', *The Listener* 69 (March 1963), p. 441

KELLER, H. 'Elgar the progressive', *Music Review* 18 (November 1957), pp. 294–99

KELLER, H. 'The First of the New', *Music and Musicians* 10 (June 1957), p. 17

KENNEDY, M. [Edward Elgar] in 'Adrian Boult,' London, Hamilton, 1987

KENNEDY, M. 'Elgar and the Festivals' in '250 years of the Three Choirs Festival' (ed. B.Still), Gloucester, Three Choirs Festival Association, 1977

KENNEDY, M. 'Elgar orchestral music', London, BBC Publications, 1970

KENNEDY, M. 'Elgar the Edwardian' in 'Elgar Studies' (ed. Raymond Monk), Aldershot, Scolar Press, 1990

KENNEDY, M. 'Elgar's religious beliefs', New Humanist 101 (Summer 1986), pp. 25–27

KENNEDY, M. 'The English Musical Renaissance 1880–1920', Gramophone 60 (August 1982), pp. 217–18

KENNEDY, M. 'Keep a bower quiet for us', The Spectator 270 (19 June 1993), pp. 35–36

KENNEDY, M. 'Lady Elgar', Music and Musicians 32 (September 1984), pp. 7–8

KENNEDY, M. 'Play a tune for a penny', Daily Telegraph, 21 March 1977, p. 12

KENNEDY, M. 'Portrait of Elgar', London, Oxford University Press, 1968; 2nd edition 1973; 3rd edition 1987

KENNEDY, M. [Review of Collett: An Elgar travelogue], Music and Letters 66 (January 1985), pp. 60–62

KENNEDY, M. [Review of De la Noy: Elgar the Man, 1983], Music and Letters 65 (July 1984), pp. 270–72

KENNEDY, M. [Review of Moore: Edward Elgar – a creative life, 1984], Music and Letters 66 (January 1986), pp. 53–55

KENNEDY, M. [Review of Moore: Spirit of England, 1984], Music and Letters 66 (January 1985), pp. 60–62

KENNEDY, M. [Review of Moore, Elgar: the Windflower Letters, 1989], Music and Letters 71 (August 1990), pp. 433–34

KENNEDY, M. 'Sixty years on – but still the wonderful boy', Daily Telegraph, 27 March 1993, p. xviii

KENNEDY, M. 'Some Elgar Interpreters' in 'Elgar Studies' (ed. Raymond Monk), Aldershot, Scolar Press, 1990

KENNEDY, M. and MAINE, B. 'Letters to the editor: Elgar', Musical Times 110 (February 1969), p. 152

KENT, C.J. 'Edward Elgar: a composer at work. A study of his creative processes as seen through his sketches and proof corrections' (2 volumes), Ph.D. thesis, King's College (University of London), 1978

KENT, C.J. 'Edward Elgar: A Guide to Research', New York, Garland Publishing, 1993

KENT, C.J. 'Elgar's evolution', The Listener 111 (23 February 1984), p. 36

KENT, C.J. 'Elgar's music for St.George's Church, Worcester', Annual Report of the Church Music Society no.77, 1983, pp. 12–26

KENT, C.J. [Review of Fanselau, 1974], Musical Times 115 (August 1974), pp. 661–62

KENT, C.J. [Review of Monk: Elgar Studies, 1990], Music and Letters 72 (August 1991), pp. 467–68

KENYON, M. 'New recordings: Elgar', Choir 55 (January 1964), pp. 13–14

KENYON, M. ' A voice for all England', The Times, 22 February 1984, p. 10

KILBURN, N. 'A personal note', *Music Student* 8 (August 1916), p. 362

KING, C.W. 'Letters to the editor: The Elgar protest', *Musical Times* 72 (May 1931), pp. 443–44

KNOWLES, J. 'Elgar Interpreters on Record: a Discography', London, Elgar Society, 1977; Thames Publishing, 2nd edition, 1985

KOLODIN, I. 'Some Englishmen of note', *Saturday Review* 4 (11 June 1977), p. 21

LACE, I. 'Elgar and Eric Coates', *Elgar Society Journal* 4 (January 1986), pp. 20–23

LAFAVE, K. 'Ovation record review', *Ovation* 9 (December 1988), p. 50

LAMB, A. 'In the saleroom', *Musical Times* 117 (April 1976), p. 317

LAMB, A. 'In the saleroom', *Musical Times* 120 (March 1979), p. 244

LAMBERT, S. [Edward Elgar] *in* 'Music Criticisms' (ed. N.Cardus), London, Oxford University Press, 1929

LEAVER, E.B. 'Some impressions of Edward Elgar', *Musical Opinion* 57 (June 1934), pp. 770–771; (July 1934), pp. 869–70

LENG, J. 'Letters to the editor: the Elgar protest', *Musical Times* 72 (June 1931), pp. 542–43

LEWIS, G.H. 'Elgar and Granville Bantock; a portrait of an unusual friendship', *Elgar Society Journal* 1 (May 1980), pp. 9–12 (Part 1); (September 1980), pp. 11–13 (Part 2)

LEWIS, G.H. 'Henry Coward (1849–1944)', *Elgar Society Journal* 2 (September 1982), pp. 11–13 ; 3 (January 1983), pp. 11–18

LLOYD, S. 'Elgar as Conductor' *in* 'An Elgar Companion' (ed. C. Redwood), Ashbourne, Sequoia, 1982

LORENZ, R. 'Letters to the editor: the Elgar protest', *Musical Times* 72 (June 1931), p. 542

LORENZ, R. 'Letters to the editor: the neglect of Elgar', *Musical Times* 64 (September 1923), p. 642

LOVELAND, K. 'Three Choirs', *Musical Times* 125 (November 1984), pp. 659–660

LOWE-DUGMORE, R. 'Delius and Elgar: a postscript', *Studies in Music* [Australia] 8 (1974), pp. 92–100

MACGREGOR, S.A. 'Elgar and the cyclical form, a study of the two symphonies', Ph.D. thesis, Queen's College, Cambridge, in preparation

MACKENZIE, C. [Editorial, with portrait], *Gramophone* 35 (June 1957), pp. 1–2

MACKENZIE, C. 'Recording in the old days', *New York Times* 106 (Section 2), 21 July 1957, p. 12

MACKENZIE, C. 'Sir Edward Elgar' *in* 'Echoes', London, Chatto and Windus, 1954

MACKERRAS, C. 'The Elgar centenary', *Canon* 10 (July 1957), pp. 385–87

McNAUGHT, W. 'Elgar', London, Novello, 1947

McNAUGHT, W. 'Elgar's birthplace', *Musical Times* 88 (June 1947), p. 185

McNAUGHT, W. 'London Concerts: the Elgar Festival', *Musical Times* 74 (January 1933), pp. 70–77

McNAUGHT, W. [Review of W.R.Anderson: Introduction to the music of Elgar], *Musical Times* 91 (September 1950), p. 345

McNAUGHT, W. [Review of Dunhill, 1938], *Music and Letters* 20 (January 1939), pp. 80–82

McNAUGHT, W. [Review of Powell: Edward Elgar – memories of a Variation. 2nd edition, 1947], *Musical Times* 88 (November 1947), p. 355

McVEAGH, D. 'Composer of the Month: Edward Elgar', *BBC Music Magazine* 2 (January 1994), pp. 39–42

McVEAGH, D. Edward Elgar *in* 'The New Grove's Dictionary of Music and Musicians' 6th edition (ed. Stanley Sadie,) London, Macmillan, 1980 Volume 6, pp. 114–130

McVEAGH, D. Edward Elgar *in* 'The New Grove Twentieth Century English Masters', London, Macmillan, 1986, pp. 1–65

McVEAGH, D. 'Edward Elgar: his life and music', London, Dent, 1955

McVEAGH, D. 'Elgar firsts', *Gramophone* 64 (May 1987), p. 1223

McVEAGH, D. 'Elgar new to London', *Musical Times* 108 (May 1967), pp. 438–39

McVEAGH, D. 'Elgar: the record for posterity', *British Institute of Recorded Sound Bulletin* no.5 (Summer 1957), pp. 9–19

McVEAGH, D. 'Elgar's birthplace', *Musical Times* 98 (June 1957), pp. 308–310

McVEAGH, D. 'Elgar's post-war passport', *Royal College of Music Magazine* 53 (June 1957), pp. 34–37

McVEAGH, D. 'Festivals', *Musical Times* 109 (September 1968), p. 833

McVEAGH, D. 'A Man's Attitude to Life' *in* 'Edward Elgar: Music and Literature' (ed. Raymond Monk), Aldershot, Scolar Press, 1993

McVEAGH, D. 'Mrs Edward Elgar', *Musical Times* 125 (February 1984), pp. 76–78

McVEAGH, D. 'Orchestral: the Imperial Elgar' *Musical Times* 116 (December 1975), p. 1079

McVEAGH, D. [Review of Burley/Carruthers], *Musical Times* 113 (November 1972), pp. 1086+1088

McVEAGH, D. [Review of Moore: Elgar–a life in photographs, 1972], *Musical Times* 114 (June 1973), pp. 599–600

McVEAGH, D. [Review of Webb: A curator's notebook], *Musical Times* 111 (March 1970), p. 283

McVEAGH, D. [Review of Young: Alice Elgar, 1978], *Musical Times* 121 (March 1980), p. 177

McVEAGH, D. 'Tewkesbury', *Musical Times* 119 (August 1978), p. 704

MAINE, B. Edward Elgar: his life and works' (2 volumes), London, Bell, 1933

MAINE, B. [Elgar] *in* 'Twang with our music', London, Epworth Press, 1946

MAINE, B. 'Elgar's sketches in relation to musicology' *in* 'Basil Maine on Music', London, Westhouse, 1946

MAINE, B. 'Letters to the editor: Elgar and Jaeger', *Musical Times* 75 (May 1934), p. 452

MAINE, B. 'Letters to the editor: Mr. Maine and Elgar', *Musical Times* 73 (April 1932), p. 354

MAINE, B. 'Letters to the editor: Mr. Maine and Elgar', *Musical Times* 73 (June 1932), p. 545

MAINE, B. 'Seven authors in search of a composer' *in* 'Basil Maine on Music', London, Westhouse, 1946

MARCH, I. 'The Gramophone collection: the orchestral music of Elgar', *Gramophone* 55 (February 1978), pp. 1381–82

MARKSON, L. 'The Elgar Edition', *Records and Recordings* 13 (January 1970), pp. 22–23

MASON, D.G. 'A great English musician', *The Outlook*, 23 August 1916, pp. 967–72

MASON, D.G. 'A study of Elgar', *Music Quarterly* 3 (April 1917), pp. 288–303

MASON, E. 'Carice Elgar', *Music and Musicians* 19 (September 1970), p. 49

MASON, E. 'Discounts on Elgar,' *Music and Musicians* 19 (November 1970), p. 50

MASON, G. 'Sir Edward Elgar' *in* 'Contemporary Composers', New York, Macmillan, 1918

MASSEY, B.S. 'The hymn tunes of Elgar and Holst', *Hymn S* 10 no.8 (1984), pp. 185–88

MELLERS, W. 'The Heart of the Matter', *Musical Times* 134 (November 1993), pp. 644–46

MENUHIN, Y. 'Impressions – Musical and Personal' *in* 'Edward Elgar Centenary Sketches' (ed. H.A.Chambers), London, Novello, 1957

MENUHIN, Y. 'Sir Edward Elgar: my musical grandfather', London, Elgar Society, 1976

MITCHELL, D. 'The composer among the monuments', *Times Literary Supplement*, 14 September 1984, pp. 1011–12

MITCHELL, D. 'Elgar and the English oratorio', *The Listener* 57 (1957), p. 361

MITCHELL, D. 'Functional vulgarity', *Musical Opinion* 79 (January 1956), p. 225

MITCHELL, D. [Review of McVeagh: Edward Elgar – his life and music, 1955], *Musical Times* 96 (December 1955), pp. 638–39

MITCHELL, D. [Review of Young: Elgar, O.M., 1955], *Musical Times* 96 (December 1955), pp. 638–39

MITCHELL, D. 'Some thoughts on Elgar (1857–1934)', *Music and Letters* 38 (April 1957), pp. 113–23

MITCHELL, D. 'Unheard music of the heart', *Times Literary Supplement*, 26 May 1989, pp. 587–89

MITCHELL, K.D. 'Elgar and Bliss', *Elgar Society Newsletter* no.9 (May 1976), pp. 32–34

MITCHELL, K.D. 'Elgar and Hardy: the projected opera', *Elgar Society Journal* 3 (September 1984), pp. 13–15

MITCHELL, W.R. 'Elgar and the Yorkshire Dales,' Settle, Castleberg, 1987

MITCHELL, W.R. 'The Giggleswick scores of Edward Elgar', Settle, Castleberg, [1990]

MOERAN, E.J. 'Letters to the editor: Elgar and the public', *Musical Times* 72 (March 1931), p. 254

MONK, R. (ed.) 'Edward Elgar: Music and Literature', Aldershot, Scolar Press, 1993

MONK, R. (ed.) 'Elgar Studies', Aldershot, Scolar Press, 1990

MOORE, E.N. 'A study of the vocal works of Sir Edward Elgar,' Ph.D. thesis, University of Rochester, 1961

MOORE, J.N. 'An Elgar discography', *Recorded Sound* 2 no.9 (1963): whole issue

MOORE, J.N. 'An international heritage', *Records and Recordings* 20 (November 1976). pp. 20–21

MOORE, J.N. 'Edward Elgar: a Creative Life', Oxford, Oxford University Press, 1984

MOORE, J.N. 'Edward Elgar: Letters of a Lifetime', Oxford, Clarendon Press, 1990

MOORE, J.N. 'Edward Elgar, the Windflower Letters', Oxford, Clarendon Press, 1989

MOORE, J.N. (ed.) [Elgar] in 'Music and Friends: seven decades of letters to Adrian Boult', London, Hamilton, 1979

MOORE, J.N. 'Elgar: A Life in Photographs', London, Oxford University Press, 1972

MOORE, J.N. 'Elgar and his Publishers' Volume 1: 1885–1903; Volume 2: 1904–1934, Oxford, Clarendon Press, 1987

MOORE, J.N. 'Elgar as a university professor', Musical Times 101 October 1960, pp. 630–31; November 1960, pp. 690–92

MOORE, J.N. 'Elgar on Record: the composer and the gramophone', London, Oxford University Press, 1974

MOORE, J.N. 'Elgar's letters to his publishers', Musical Times 125 (January 1984), pp. 16–18

MOORE, J.N. [Introduction to Volume 1 of The Elgar Edition: the Complete Electrical Recordings of Sir Edward Elgar], London, E.M.I., 1992

MOORE, J.N. 'The Music of Youth and Age' in Volume 2 of The Elgar Edition:the Complete Electrical Recordings of Sir Edward Elgar, London, E.M.I., 1992

MOORE, J.N. 'Spirit of England' London, Heinemann, 1984

MOORE, J.N. 'The Time Machine' in Volume 3 of The Elgar Edition: the Complete Electrical Recordings of Sir Edward Elgar, London, E.M.I.,1993

MOORE, J.N. 'Young Elgar at the Festival' in 'An Elgar Companion' (ed. C. Redwood), Ashbourne, Sequoia, 1982

MOORE, J.N. and KENNEDY, M. 'Edward Elgar and Ralph Vaughan Williams' in 'Heritage in Music' (volume 4), edited by M.Raeburn and A.Kendall, Oxford, Oxford University Press, 1989

MORRISON, R. 'Tunes for a land of bold hope and shabby glory', The Times Supplement, 13 July 1991, pp. 16–17

MUNDY, S. 'Elgar: his life and times', London, Midas Books, 1980

MYERS, C. 'British organ music', Musical Opinion 112 (June 1989), pp. 192–94

NEEL, B. 'Edward Elgar 1857–1934', Canadian Music Journal 1 (Summer 1957), pp. 27–32

NEWMAN, E. 'The Artist and the Man', The Sunday Times, 13 October 1955, p. 7

NEWMAN, E. 'The Changing Elgar', The Sunday Times, 25 November 1956, p. 13

NEWMAN, E. 'Edward Elgar: no.2 in The New School of British Music', The Speaker (new series) 5 (21 December 1901), pp. 331–32

NEWMAN, E. 'Elgar', London, J.Lane/Bodley Head, 1906

NEWMAN, E. 'Elgar: some aspects of the Man and his Music', The Sunday Times, 25 February 1934, p. 5

NEWMAN, E. 'Elgar Memories', The Sunday Times, 30 October 1955, p. 7

NEWMAN, E. 'A famous contemporary sums up Elgar', Musical America 77 (February 1957), pp. 3–4+

NEWMAN, E. 'The Final Elgar', The Sunday Times, 9 December 1956, p. 6

NEWMAN, E. 'Readings of Elgar', *The Sunday Times*, 6 November 1955, p. 7

NEWMAN, E. 'Stately Sorrow', *The Listener* 51 (11 March 1954), pp. 421–422

NEWTON, R.F. 'Additional details of tune composers', *Hymn S.* 6 no.8 (1967), p. 160

NORTHCOTT, B. 'Making tracks for Elgar', *The Independent*, 23 May 1992, p. 33

NORTHCOTT, B. 'A rousing clash of symbols', *The Independent*, 1 January 1994, p. 45

NOTCUTT, A. 'Recollections of some early Elgar performances', *Musical Opinion* 74 (October 1950), pp. 9+

O'CALLAGHAN, J. 'Elgar: a Herefordshire Guide', *London, Unipress*, 1985

O'CALLAGHAN, J. 'Elgar's letters to Sir Percy Hull', Hereford Three Choirs Festival Programme Book, 1991

ORR, C.W. 'Elgar and the Public', *Musical Times* 72 (June 1931), pp. 17–18

ORR, C.W. 'Letters to the editor: The neglect of Elgar', *Musical Times* 64 (August 1923), p. 569

OTTAWAY, H. 'Elgar among the hills', *The Listener* 97 (23 June 1977), p. 818

OTTAWAY, H. 'Elgar and a new generation', *Musical Opinion* 76 (October 1952), pp. 17–19

OTTAWAY, H. 'Malvern', *Musical Times* 119 (August 1978), p. 704

OTTAWAY, H. 'The Malvern Elgar Festival', *Musical Opinion* 74 (November–December 1950), p. 67+

OTTAWAY, H. 'The Malvern Elgar Festival', *Musical Opinion* 74 (July 1951), p. 521

OTTAWAY, H. [Review of Young (ed.): Edward Elgar – Letters to Nimrod: Edward Elgar to August Jaeger, 1965], *Musical Times* 106 (November 1965), pp. 860–61

PARKER, C. 'Recording Elgar's choral works', *Gramophone* 55 (June 1977), pp. 23–24

PARMENTER, R. 'Elgar homage', *The New York Times* 106 Section 2 (13 January 1957), p. 9

PARROTT, I. 'Elgar', London, Dent, 1971

PARROTT, I. 'Elgar and Bach', *Elgar Society Newsletter* no. 9 (May 1976), pp. 26–29

PARROTT, I. 'Elgar's enigma solved', *Delius* no.76 (July 1982), pp. 21–22

PARROTT, I. 'Elgar's Harmonic Language' *in* 'Elgar Studies' (ed. Raymond Monk), Aldershot, Scolar Press, 1990

PARROTT, I. 'Elgar's two-fold enigma: a religious sequel', *Music and Letters* 54 (January 1973), pp. 57–60

PARROTT, I. 'Was Elgar's orchestration impeccable?' *The Chesterian* 32 (Summer 1957), pp. 20–23

PATTERSON, A. 'Great Minds in Music', *Great Thoughts* 7, pp. 8–10

PAYNE, A. 'A new look at Elgar', *The Listener* 72 (29 October 1964), p. 694

PHILIP, R. 'The recordings of Edward Elgar (1857–1934): Authenticity and Performance Practice', *Early Music* 12 (November 1984), pp. 481–489

PHILLIPS, J.C. 'The Elgar Statue,' *Musical Times* 121 (July 1980), p. 440

PIRIE, P.J. 'Bantock and his generation', *Musical Times* 109 (August 1968), pp. 715–17

PIRIE, P.J. 'Crippled splendour: Elgar and Mahler', *Musical Times* 97 (February 1956), pp. 70–71

PIRIE, P.J. 'Debussy and English music', *Musical Times* 108 (July 1967), pp. 599–601

PIRIE, P. J. 'Delius and Elgar', *Music and Musicians* 23 (July 1975), pp. 35–37

PIRIE, P.J. 'Elgar and the orchestra', *Music and Musicians* 27 (January 1979), pp. 26–28

PIRIE, P.J. 'The personality of Elgar', *Music and Musicians* 21 (April 1973), pp. 32–36

PIRIE, P.J. [Review of Hurd, 1969], *Musical Times* 110 (May 1969), pp. 491–92

PIRIE, P.J. [Review of Kennedy: Portrait of Elgar, 1968], *Musical Times* 109 (August 1968), pp. 728–29

PIRIE, P.J. [Review of Young (ed.): A future of English music and other lectures, 1968], *Musical Times* 109 (August 1968), pp. 728–29

PIRIE, P.J. 'World's end: a study of Edward Elgar', *Music Review* 18 (May 1957), pp. 89–100

POLYBANK, C. 'Elgar, Parry, Stanford and the Brahms connection', M.Phil. thesis, University of Reading, in preparation

PORTE, J.F. 'Elgar and his music: an appreciative story', London, Pitman, 1933

PORTE, J.F. 'Letters to the editor: the Elgar protest', *Musical Times* 72 (June 1931), p. 543

PORTE, J.F. 'Sir Edward Elgar', London, Kegan Paul, 1921

POWELL, D.M. 'Back to '95: some memories of Elgar', *British Institute of Recorded Sound Bulletin* no.5 (Summer 1957), pp. 2–9

POWELL, D.M. 'Edward Elgar: Memories of a Variation', London, Oxford University Press, 1937; 2nd ed. 1947; 3rd ed. 1979; 4th ed. (with an introduction by Claud Powell and appendices revised by Jerrold Northrop Moore), Scolar Press, 1994

POWELL, D.M. 'Letters to the editor: Elgariana' *Musical Times* 97 (March 1956), p. 146

POWELL, D.M. 'The Music Maker' *in* 'Edward Elgar Centenary Sketches', (ed. H.A. Chambers) London, Novello, 1957

RAWLINSON, H. 'Edward Elgar – violinist', *Strad* 65 (May 1954), p. 8+; (June 1954), p. 44+; (July 1954), p. 76+; (August 1954), p. 110+; (October 1954), p. 176+; (November 1954), p. 220+

RAWLINSON, H. 'Elgar and Romberg's violin duets', *Strad* 68 (July 1957), pp. 88–89

RAYNOR, H. 'Elgar and Englishness', *Musical Opinion* 80 (June 1957), p. 527+

READ, J. 'Correspondence: documentary Elgar', *Gramophone* 49 (November 1971), p. 952

REDLICH, H. 'In Memoriam', *Musica* 11 (June 1957), pp. 353–54

REDWOOD, C. 'Delius and Elgar: a Midlands branch talk', *Delius* no.103 (Winter 1990), p. 20

REDWOOD, C. 'Elgar and Delius' *in* 'An Elgar Companion' (ed. C. Redwood), Ashbourne, Sequoia, 1982

REDWOOD, C. (ed.) 'An Elgar Companion', Ashbourne, Sequoia, 1982

REED, N. 'Elgar's enigmatic inamorata', *Musical Times* 125 (August 1984), pp. 430–434

REED, W.H. 'Elgar', London, Dent, 1939

REED, W.H. 'Elgar as I knew him', London, Gollancz, 1936

REES, C.B. 'Elgar', *London Music* 12 (May 1957), pp. 21–23

REES, C.B. 'Musical roundabout', *Music Teacher* 34 (November 1955), p. 533

REID, C. 'Elgar: a recantation', *Philharmonic Post* 6 (May–June 1953), pp. 98–99

RIDOUT, G. 'Elgar: the angular Saxon', *Canadian Music Journal* 1 (Summer 1957), pp. 33–34

ROBINSON, S. 'Elgar's Light Music' *in* 'Elgar Centenary Sketches' (ed. H.A. Chambers), London, Novello, 1957

ROSENWALD, H. 'Contemporary music', *Music News* 42 (December 1950), p. 6

RUBBRA, E. [Review of Reed: Elgar as I knew him, 1936], *Music and Letters* 18 (January 1937), p. 78

RUSHTON, J. 'Edward Elgar', *Music and Musicians* 22 (February 1974), pp. 18–21

RUTLAND, H. 'Elgarian notes and comments' *Musical Times* 98 (June 1957), p. 310

SADIE, J.A. 'At home with the masters', *Gramophone* 71 (October 1993), p. 11

SALTER, L.[Review:McVeagh-Twentieth century English masters,1986], *Musical Times* 128 (January 1987), pp. 24–25

SAMPSON, G. 'Sir Edward Elgar', *The Bookman*, March 1921, pp. 218–220

SAMS, E. 'Elgar's cipher letter to Dorabella', *Musical Times* 111 (February 1970), pp. 151–54

SAMS, E. 'Elgar's Enigmas: a past script and a post script', *Musical Times* 111 (July 1970), pp. 692–94

SANDERS, A. 'The Elgar Edition: the acoustic HMV recordings', *Gramophone* 70 (September 1992), pp. 168–69

SANDERS, A. 'The Elgar Edition, volume 1', *Gramophone* 70 (June 1992), pp. 90+92

SANDERS. A. 'The Elgar Edition, volume 2', *Gramophone* 70 (February 1993), p. 79

SANDERS, A. 'The Elgar Edition, volume 3', *Gramophone* 71 (August 1993), pp. 89–90

SARGENT, M. 'Elgar – As I knew him', *Music and Musicians* 10 (June 1957), p. 13

SCHOLES, P.A. 'Elgar and the War', *Music Student* 8 (August 1916), pp. 357–358

SCHOLES,P.M. 'Elgar at Severn House – II', *Music Student* 8 (August 1916), pp. 343–348

SCHOLES, P.M. 'Our Greatest British Composer', *Youth and Music* 2, pp. 73–76

SCHOLES, P.M. 'Sir Edward Elgar', *Everyman* 3 (13 March 1914), pp. 716–17

SCHOLES, P.M. 'Sir Edward Elgar: Introductory Sketch', *Music Student* 8 (August 1916), pp. 335–337

SCHONBERG, H.C. 'Elgar', *New York Times* 106 Section 2 (2 June 1957), p. 14

SCOWCROFT, P.L. 'Elgar and Folk Song', *Elgar Society Journal* 4 (May 1985), p. 14

SELF, G. [Elgar] *in* 'Julius Harrison and the importunate muse', Aldershot, Scolar Press, 1993

SENIOR, E. 'Elgar museum', *Music and Musicians* 17 (October 1968), p. 40

SHARP, G. 'A note on Elgar's music', *Music Review* 18 (May 1957), pp. 106–8

SHAW, A.T. 'Elgar's birthplace reopened', *Musical Times* 108 (July 1957), pp. 607–8

SHAW, G.B. [Elgar], *Musical Times* 70 (September 1929), p. 807

SHELDON, A.J. 'Edward Elgar', London, 'Musical Opinion', 1932

SHENTON, K. 'Elgar and William Wolstenholme', *Elgar Society Journal* 8 (May 1994), pp. 200–207

SHEPPHERD, L. 'Elgar as a violinist', *Strad* 92 (November 1981), pp. 501–4

SHERA, F.H. 'Elgar: Instrumental Works', London, Oxford University Press, 1931

SHORE, B. 'Edward Elgar (1857–1934)', *Gramophone* 35 (June 1957), pp. 2+4

SHAW, G.B. 'Edward Elgar', *Music and Letters* 1 (January 1920), pp. 7–11

SHAW, H.W. [Elgar] *in* 'The Three Choirs Festival', Worcester, Baylis, 1954

SIMMONS, D. 'Recent records', *Strad* 88 (August 1977), pp. 341+

SIMMONS, K. and M. 'The Elgars of Worcester', New Barnet, Elgar Society, 1984

SIMMONS, K. and M. 'A walk round Elgar's Worcester', *Elgar Society Journal* 4 (May 1985), pp. 7–13; (September 1985), pp. 18–26; (January 1986), pp. 8–20

SORABJI, K. 'Letters to the editor: The Elgar protest', *Musical Times* 72 (May 1931), p. 444

SPEED, K. 'Elgar: a world genius', *Daily Telegraph*, 4 January 1993, p. 16

SPEYER, E. [Elgar] *in* 'My life and friends', London, Cobden-Sanderson, 1937

STACEY, G. 'Bibliography of Elgar', *Musical Times* 90 (July 1949), pp. 246

STACEY, G. 'Letters to the editor: Elgar nieces', *Musical Times* 90 (July 1949), p. 246

STANFIELD, M.B. 'Silhouettes from Britain', *Violins* 10 (August-September 1949), pp. 230–1

STEVENS, R. 'The cyclic principle: unifying procedures in romantic instrumental music from Beethoven to Elgar', M.A. thesis, University of Birmingham, 1983

STEVENSON, P. 'A visit to Elgar's birthplace', *Musical Times* 83 (October 1942), pp. 297–99

STEVENSON, R. 'Whimsy and Spleen', *The Listener* 85 (3 June 1971), p. 730

STOCKLEY, W.C. 'Introducing Sir Edward Elgar' *in* 'Fifty years of music in Birmingham 1850–1900', Birmingham, Hudson, 1913

STREATFEILD, R.A. 'An English Musician: Edward Elgar' [The Hague, unable to trace any publisher, 1912] According to the British Museum catalogue, a version in Italian was published in Rome, 1912, and a version in Danish in Copenhagen, 1914.

STREATFEILD, R.A. [Symphonic music: Elgar], *Musical Times* 53 (June 1912), pp. 386–87

STRONG, R. 'Pomp and new circumstance', *The Times*, 31 March 1984, p. 8

SUMSION, H. 'Elgar: some personal recollections', *Royal College of Music Magazine* 80 no.3 (1984), pp. 127–29

SURTEES-TALBOT, G.C. 'Elgar as a writer of church anthems', *Music Student* 8 (August 1916), p. 364

TAYLOR, R. 'Music in the Air: Elgar and the B.B.C.' *in* 'Edward Elgar: Music and Literature' (ed. Raymond Monk), Aldershot, Scolar Press, 1993

TAYLOR, R. 'Shaw and Elgar' *in* 'Elgar Studies' (ed. Raymond Monk), Aldershot, Scolar Press, 1990

TERNANT, A. de 'Letters to the editor: The neglect of Elgar', *Musical Times* 64 (October 1923), p. 722

TERRY, R. 'Elgar as I knew him', *Radio Times*, 9 March 1934, p. 710

TOPPING, G. 'Biking has begun!' *BBC Music Magazine* 2 (January 1994), pp. 42–43

TOVEY, D.F. [Edward Elgar] *in* 'Some English Symphonists' London, Oxford University Press, 1941

TOVEY, D.F. 'Elgar, Master of Music', *Music and Letters* 16 (January 1935), pp. 1–4

TRAHAIR, C.A. and J.F. 'Elgar's church music: a discussion', *Journal of Musiological Research* 8 nos.3/4 (1989), pp. 313–31

TROWELL, B. 'Elgar's Marginalia', *Musical Times* 125 (March 1984), pp. 139–43

TROWELL, B. 'Elgar's Songs as Contrfacta: Some lost and unknown songs recovered' in 'Sundry Sorts of Music Books' London, The British Library, 1993

TROWELL, B. 'Elgar's Use of Literature' *in* 'Edward Elgar: Music and Literature' (ed. Raymond Monk), Aldershot, Scolar Press, 1993

TURNER, E.O. 'Tempo Variation: with examples from Elgar', *Music and Letters* 19 (July 1938), pp. 308–23

TURNER, W.J. 'Elgar and Handel' *in* 'An Elgar Companion' (ed. C. Redwood), Ashbourne, Sequoia, 1982

VALE, H. 'Letters to the editor: Mr.Edward Elgar's biographical sketch,' *Musical Times* 41 (November 1900), p. 750

VANSON, F. 'Elgar', *Strad* 91 (November 1980), p. 496

VARIOUS 'Elgar today: a symposium,' *Musical Times* 98 (June 1957), pp. 302–7

VARIOUS 'Letters to the editor: Elgar's birthplace as a memorial', *Musical Times* 76 (October 1935), p. 933

VARIOUS 'Letters to the editor: Mr. Maine and Elgar', *Musical Times* 73 (March 1932), p. 259

VARIOUS 'Letters to the editor: Mr. Maine and Elgar', *Musical Times* 73 (May 1932), p. 450

VARIOUS 'Tribute and Commentary', *Musical Times* 75 (April 1934), pp. 320–22

VINCE, S. 'Unfinished works', *Musical Opinion* 76 (December 1952), pp. 151+

VOLBACH, F. 'Edward Elgar' [Translations], *Elgar Society Journal* 5 (January 1987), pp. 4–8; (May 1987), pp. 4–8

VOLBACH, W. 'Edward Elgar and Fritz Volbach', *Musical Opinion* 60 (July 1937), pp. 870–72. Reprinted in *Elgar Society Journal* 5 (September 1988), pp. 4–10

WAITE, V. 'Elgar as conductor', *Elgar Society Newsletter* no. 5 (January 1975), pp. 23–26.

WAITE, V. 'Elgar, the letter writer', *Musical Opinion* 103 (July 1980), pp. 398–400+403

WALDEN, G. 'Who let these second-raters sneak into the hall of fame?' *Daily Telegraph*, 2 January 1993, p. 14

WALKER, M. [Review of Knowles, 1985], *Gramophone* 64 (October 1986), p. 528

WALTER, A. 'From 78 to CD' (Volume 3: The Elgar Edition – The Complete Electronic Recordings of Sir Edward Elgar), London, E.M.I., [1993]

WARRACK, J. 'Three English masters', *Gramophone* 61 (March 1984), pp. 1059–60

WEAVER, C. 'The Thirteenth Enigma?' London, Thames, 1989

WEBB, A. 'A curator's notebook', Broadheath (Worcester), Elgar Birthplace Trust, 1970

WEBB, A. 'Some personal memories', *Elgar Society Newsletter* no.3 (May 1974), pp. 21–22

WEBBER, J. LLOYD 'Elgar: a world genius', *Daily Telegraph*, 4 January 1993, p. 16

WELLS-HARRISON, W. 'Elgar's shorter orchestral works', *Music Student* 8 (August 1916), pp. 354–356

WESTRUP, J.A. 'Elgar and Joseph Bennett' *in* 'Sharps and Flats', London, Oxford University Press, 1940

WESTRUP, J.A. [Letter about Elgar's style], *Elgar Society Newsletter* no.2 (January 1974), p. 24

WESTRUP, J.A. [Review of McNaught, 1947], *Musical Times* 88 (October 1947), p. 320

WESTRUP, J.A.[Review of Moore:Elgar – a life in photographs,1972], *Music and Letters* 54 (April 1973), p. 237

WESTRUP, J.A. [Review of Young (ed.): Letters to Nimrod, 1965], *Music and Letters* 47 (January 1966), pp. 61–63

WHITAKER–WILSON, C. 'Elgar, composer and conductor', *Musical Opinion* 34 (February 1911), p. 327

WHITWELL, D. 'Twentieth century English composers – their music for winds', *Instrument* 23 (November 1968), pp. 47–48

WILLCOCKS, D. 'A Modern View' *in* 'Edward Elgar Centenary Sketches' (ed. H.A.Chambers), London, Novello, 1957

WILLETTS, P.J. 'The Elgar Sketch Books', *British Library Journal* 11 (Spring 1985), pp. 25–45

WILLIAMS, R.VAUGHAN 'What have we learnt from Elgar?' *Music and Letters* 16 (January 1935), pp. 13–19

WILLIAMS, S. 'The Elgar centenary', *The New York Times* 106 Section 7 (2 June 1957), p. 2

WILSON, C.R. 'Elgar, Naylor and The Cobbler's Jig: a enquiry re-opened', *Music and Letters* 74 (February 1993), pp. 39–43

WILSON, S. 'Some reminiscences of Elgar', *Elgar Society Newsletter* no. 6 (new series), September 1978, pp. 7–11

WIMBUSH, R. 'Here and there', *Gramophone* 50 (January 1973), pp. 1313–14

WINTERNITZ, E. [Elgar] *in* 'Musical autographs from Monteverdi to Hindemith', New York, Dover Publications, 1965 (2 volumes)

WOHLFELD, H.S. 'Carice Irene Blake: memories 1941–1970', *Elgar Society Journal* 6 (May 1990), pp. 8–9

WOOD, F. 'Edward Elgar', *Music in Education*, May–June 1944, pp. 54–5

WOOD, H.J [Edward Elgar] in 'My Life of Music', London, Gollancz, 1938

WOODFIELD, R. 'Letters to the editor: Edward Elgar', *Musical Opinion* 62 (December 1938), p. 238 ; (February 1939), p. 434

WRATTEN, B. 'Correspondence: Elgar at Hereford', *Gramophone* 50 (November 1972), p. 1038

WRIGHT, N. 'Sir Edward Elgar', *Cathedral Choirmaster* 43 (Fall 1957), pp. 109–110+

WRIGHT, P. 'Records: Elgar', *Music and Musicians* 25 (July 1977), pp. 36–37

YOUNG,P.M. 'Alice Elgar: Enigma of a Victorian Lady' London, Dobson, 1978

YOUNG, P.M. 'Edward Elgar: music for the Catholic liturgy', *American Choral Review* 28 no.1 (1986), pp. 3–10

YOUNG, P.M. 'Edward Elgar and John Henry Newman', Worcester Three Choirs Festival Programme Book, 1990

YOUNG, P.M. 'Elgar, O.M.: a study of a musician', London, Collins, 1955

YOUNG, P.M. 'Elgar as a Man of Letters' in 'Edward Elgar Centenary Sketches' (ed. H.A.Chambers), London, Novello, 1957

YOUNG, P.M. (ed.) ' A future of English music and other lectures by Edward Elgar', London, Dobson, 1968

YOUNG, P.M. 'Letters: Elgar and Rosa' – reply to P.J.Pirie *Music and Musicians* 21 (June 1973), pp. 4–5

YOUNG, P.M. (ed.) 'Letters of Edward Elgar and other writings', London, Bles, 1956

YOUNG,P.M. 'Letters to Nimrod: Edward Elgar to August Jaeger, 1897–1908', London, Dobson, 1965

YOUNG, P.M. [Review of Atkins: The Elgar–Atkins Friendship, 1984], *Music and Letters* 66 (January 1985), pp. 55–56

GOD SAVE THE KING

ANON. 'Reviews', *Musical Times* 43 (December 1902), p. 809

GRANIA AND DIARMID (Op. 42)

ANON. 'London Concerts: Queen's Hall', *Musical Times* 43 (February 1902), p. 116

ANON. 'Reviews', *Musical Times* 44 (November 1903), p. 739

KENNEDY, M. Sleeve note for ASD 3050 (1975)

MOORE, J.N. 'Grania and Diarmid: Funeral March', *Gramophone* 52 (February 1975), p. 1491

YOUNG, P. M. 'Elgar and the Irish Dramatists' in 'Edward Elgar: Music and Literature' (ed. Raymond Monk), Aldershot, Scolar Press, 1993

GREAT IS THE LORD

KENNEDY, M. 'Great is the Lord', *Gramophone* 64 (March 1987), pp. 1309–10
MOORE, J.N. Sleeve note for CDC7 47658–2 (1987)

IMPERIAL MARCH (Op. 32)

ANON. [Announcements], *Musical Times* 38 (August 1897), p. 554
ANON. 'Reviews', *Musical Times* 38 (April 1897), p. 249
ROBERTSON, A. 'Imperial March', *Gramophone* 31 (July 1953), p. 38
SARGENT, M. Sleeve note for LXT 2793 (1953)

IN THE SOUTH (Op. 50)

ANON. [In the South], *Chicago Symphony Orchestra Program Notes*, 4 November 1965, p. 4+
HODGKINS, G. 'Elgar's notes on In the South', *Elgar Society Journal* 5 (January 1987), pp. 14–20
KREHBIEL, H.E. 'Cincinnati Music Festival and Sir Edward Elgar', *Musical Times* 47 (June 1906), p. 396
PITT, P. and KALISCH, A. 'In the South. Analytical and Descriptive Notes', London, Novello, 1904
TOVEY, D.F. In the South (Alassio) in 'Essays in Musical Analysis' Volume 6: Miscellaneous Notes, London, Oxford University Press, 1935–39

INTRODUCTION AND ALLEGRO (Op. 47)

ANON. 'Editorial notes', *Strad* 84 (September 1973), p. 311
ANON. [Introduction and Allegro], *Boston Symphony Orchestra Program Notes*, 11 March 1966, pp. 1171+
ANON. [Introduction and Allegro], *Detroit Symphony Orchestra Program Notes*, 18 December 1969, pp. 297–301
ANON. 'The London Symphony Orchestra: an Elgar Concert', *Musical Times* 46 (April 1905), p. 259
ELGAR, E.W. Programme note for the first performance of the 'Introduction and Allegro for Strings' (Op. 47): 8 March 1905
MACDONALD, M. 'Introduction and Allegro,' *Gramophone* 35 (June 1957), pp. 9–10
McVEAGH, D. 'Moriah and the Introduction and Allegro', *Elgar Society Journal* 4 (January 1986), pp. 23–24
SHORE, B. 'Edward Elgar 1857–1934', *Gramophone* 35 (June 1957), pp. 3–4
TOVEY, D.F. Introduction and Allegro in 'Essays in Musical Analysis' Volume 6: Miscellaneous Notes, London, Oxford University Press, 1935–39

KING ARTHUR

MARCH, I. 'King Arthur', *Gramophone* 71 (November 1993), p. 168
SALTER, L. 'King Arthur', *Gramophone* 51 (January 1974), pp. 1372+7
WALKER, M. Sleeve note for CHAN 6582 (1993)
YOUNG, P. M. Sleeve note for Polydor 2383 224
See also under *Arthur*

THE KINGDOM (Op. 51)

ACHENBACH, A. 'The Kingdom,' *Gramophone* 71 (June 1993), p. 83
ANDERSON, R. 'Elgar's Magus and Projector' *in* 'Elgar Studies' (ed. Raymond Monk), Aldershot, Scolar Press, 1990
ANON. 'The Birmingham Festival', *Musical Times* 47 (November 1906), pp. 757–58
ANON. [Elgar's The Kingdom], *Mens en Melodie* 8 (February 1953), pp. 54–55
ANON. 'Sir Edward Elgar's new oratorio', *Musical Times* 47 (October 1906), pp. 675–76
BONAVIA, F. 'Elgar's The Kingdom', *Musical Times* 86 (April 1945), pp. 111–112
BOULT, A.,YOUNG,P.M. and BOWEN, P. Sleeve notes for SAN 244/245 (1969)
BOWEN, M. 'Elgar's Kingdom', *Music and Musicians* 18 (May 1970), p. 60
CRANKSHAW, G. 'Kingdom come', *Records and Recordings* 12 (April 1969), pp. 24–25
DAY, E. 'Letters to the Editor: Elgar's interpretations', *Musical Times* 110 (October 1969), p. 1039
DOMMETT, K. 'Three Choirs', *Music and Musicians* 19 (November 1970), p. 30
GORTON, C.V. 'The Kingdom: an Interpretation of the Libretto', London, Novello, 1906
GROGAN, C. 'My dear analyst: some observations on Elgar's correspondence with A.J. Jaeger regarding the Apostles project', *Music and Letters* 72 (January 1991), pp. 48–60
HALL, D. 'A superb realization of Elgar's oratorio The Kingdom by Sir Adrian Boult', *Stereo Review* 36 (April 1976), pp. 77–78
JAEGER, A.J. 'Elgar's new choral works', *Musical Times* 49 (July 1908), pp. 453–54
JAEGER, A.J. 'The Kingdom: Book of Words with Analytical Notes and Descriptive Notes', London, Novello, 1906
JOHNSON, S. 'The Kingdom comes', *Gramophone* 66 (March 1989), p. 1392
KENNEDY, M. 'The Kingdom', *Gramophone* 65 (May 1988), p. 1630
KIRBY, A.J. 'The Apostles and The Kingdom' *in* 'Edward Elgar Centenary Sketches' (ed. H.A.Chambers), London, Novello, 1957
MOORE, J.N. 'Aberdeenshire', *Musical Times* 116 (July 1975), p. 648
PIRIE, P. J. 'Gramophone records: Elgar conducts Elgar', *Music Review* 33 no.1 (1972), pp. 76–80
POWELL, D.M. 'The first performances of The Apostles and The Kingdom', *Musical Times* 101 (January 1960), pp. 21–22

POWELL, D.M. 'The words of The Apostles and The Kingdom', *Musical Times* 89 (May 1948), pp. 201–204 (Part 1); 90 (May 1949), pp. 149–152 (Part 2)
ROBERTSON, A. 'The Kingdom', *Gramophone* 46 (April 1969), pp. 1453–54
ROSS, C. 'Three Choirs Festival, Worcester, August 18–25', *Musical Opinion* 108 (February 1985), pp. 151–52

LAND OF HOPE AND GLORY

ANON. 'Nostalgia?' *Musical Opinion* 93 (October 1969), pp. 5–6
BARKER, F. 'Thoughts on a tune: Land of Hope and Glory', *Encounter* 59 (November 1982), pp. 40–41
BURY, D. 'In pursuit of the forgotten obligato', *Elgar Society Journal* 3 (May 1984), pp. 11–14

THE LAST JUDGEMENT

WHITTALL, A. 'Elgar's Last Judgement', *Music Review* 26 no.1, (1965), pp. 23–27

THE LIGHT OF LIFE (LUX CHRISTI) (Op. 29)

ACHENBACH, A. 'Light of Life', *Gramophone* 70 (May 1993), pp. 82–83
ANDERSON, R. 'Worcester', *Musical Times* 126 (June 1985), pp. 140–141
ANON. 'Rare Tchaikovsky and Elgar', *Music and Musicians* 27 (November 1978), pp. 30–31
BENNETT, J. 'Some Festival Novelties', *Musical Times* 37 (September 1896), pp. 599–600
GROGAN, C. 'Elgar's high art', *Musical Times* 131 (October 1990), p. 545
HARVEY, T. 'Light of Life', *Gramophone* 58 (April 1981), pp. 1352+55
KENNEDY, M. Sleeve note for ASD 3952 (1981)
KENNEDY, M. Sleeve note for CDM7 64732–4 (1993)
MOORE, J.N. 'Light of Light: Meditation', *Gramophone* 52 (February 1975), p. 1491
NORRIS, G. 'Elgar', *Musical Times* 121 (September 1980), p. 574
PUFFETT, D. 'Radio' *Music and Musicians* 23 (June 1975), pp. 36–38

MEMORIAL CHIMES FOR A CARILLON

LAWSON, J.R. 'Edward Elgar and the carillon', *Guild of Carilloneurs in North America Bulletin* 19 (April 1968), pp. 56–58. Reprinted in *Elgar Society Journal* 3 (May 1983), pp. 19–21

MINA

FISKE, R. 'Mina', *Gramophone* 48 (November 1970), pp. 787–88
KENNEDY, M. Sleeve note for ASD 2638 (1970)

THE MUSIC MAKERS (Op. 69)

BLYTH, A. 'The Music Makers', *Gramophone* 64 (January 1987), p. 1051
HOLMES, S.C. 'Arthur O'Shaughnessy and The Music Makers', *Elgar Society Newsletter* no.5 (January 1975), pp. 26–29
LOVELAND, K. 'Worcester', *Musical Times* 122 (August 1981), p. 551
NEWMAN, E. 'The Music Makers', *Musical Times* 53 (September 1912), pp. 566–70
ROBERTSON, A. 'The Music Makers', *Gramophone* 44 (May 1967), p. 592
YOUNG, P.M. Sleeve note for ALP/ASD 2311 (1967)
YOUNG, P.M. Sleeve note for CDS7 47208–8 (1987)

NURSERY SUITE

HARVEY, T. 'Nursery Suite', *Gramophone* 32 (September 1954), pp. 149–150

O HEARKEN THOU

ANON. 'The Coronation of George V and Queen Mary in Westminster Abbey, 22 June 1911', *Musical Times* 52 (July 1911), pp. 433–37
ANON. [Review of publications], *Musical Times* 52 (November 1911), p. 725
KENNEDY, M. 'O Hearken Thou', *Gramophone* 66 (January 1989), p. 1195
KENNEDY, M. Sleeve note for CDA 66313 (1989)

PAGEANT OF EMPIRE

GRACE, H. [Review of new music], *Musical Times* 65 (October 1924), p. 917

POLONIA (Op. 76)

ANON. 'Elgar's Symphonic Prelude: Polonia. Performance at Queen's Hall', *Musical Times* 56 (August 1915), p. 491
COLLETT, B. Sleeve note for SHE CD 9602 (1988)
KENNEDY, M. Sleeve note for ASD 3050 (1975)
KENNEDY, M. Sleeve note for CDM7 69207–2 (1988)
MOORE, J.N. 'Polonia', *Gramophone* 52 (February 1975), p. 1491

SANDERS, A. 'Polonia', *Gramophone* 65 (April 1988), p. 1500
SANDERS, A. 'Polonia', *Gramophone* 65 (May 1988), p. 1628

POMP AND CIRCUMSTANCE MILITARY MARCHES No.1 in D MAJOR (Op. 39 no.1) and No.2 in A MINOR (Op. 39 no.2)

ANON. 'Music in Liverpool and District', *Musical Times* 42 (December 1901), p. 822
ANON. 'Promenade Concerts', *Musical Times* 42 (December 1901), p. 819
GOLDINE, R. Sleeve note for CDM7 64015-2 (1992)
HARVEY, T. 'Elgar Marches', *Gramophone* 34 (October 1956), p. 161
HARVEY, T. 'Elgar Marches', *Gramophone* 36 (April 1959), p. 513
JAMES, B. Sleeve note for ALP 1379 (1956)
KENNEDY, M. 'Elgar Marches', *Gramophone* 69 (April 1992), pp. 46+48
PUDNEY, D. Sleeve notes for SB2026 (1959)

QUARTET FOR STRINGS (Op. 83)

ANON. 'Elgar's new chamber music', *Musical Times* 60 (June 1919), p. 282
ANON. 'Elgar's String Quartet', *Musical Times* 60 (July 1919), pp. 336–38
COBBETT, W.W. [Quartet for Strings: Elgar] *in* 'Cobbett's Cyclopaedic Survey of Chamber Music', London, Oxford University Press, 1929
KEYS, I. 'Ghostly Stuff: The Brinkwells Music' *in* 'Edward Elgar: Music and Literature' (ed. Raymond Monk), Aldershot, Scolar Press, 1993

QUINTET FOR PIANO AND STRINGS (Op. 84)

ANON. 'Elgar's new chamber music', *Musical Times* 60 (June 1919), p. 282
ANON. 'Other recommended CDs', *Musical Opinion* 112 (December 1989), p. 422
COBBETT, W.W. [Quintet for Piano and Strings: Elgar] *in* 'Cobbett's Cyclopaedic Survey of Chamber Music', London, Oxford University Press, 1929
COLLES, H.C. 'Elgar's Quintet for Pianoforte and Strings (Op. 84)', *Musical Times* 60 (November 1919), pp. 596–600
KEYS, I. 'Ghostly Stuff: The Brinkwells Music' *in* 'Edward Elgar: Music and Literature' (ed. Raymond Monk), Aldershot, Scolar Press, 1993
STAPLES, J.G. 'Six lesser-known piano quintets of the twentieth century', D.M.A. thesis, School of Music (Rochester University), 1972

ROMANCE FOR BASSOON AND ORCHESTRA (Op. 62)

CANTRELL, S. 'Ovation record review', *Ovation* 9 (September 1988), pp. 43–45

SALUT D'AMOUR (Op. 12)

TURNER, J.R. 'Nineteenth century autograph music manuscripts in the Pierpont Morgan Library: a check list', *Nine Centuries of Music* 4 no.1 (1980) p. 66

THE SANGUINE FAN (Op. 81)

HARVEY, T. 'The Sanguine Fan', *Gramophone* 51 (March 1974), pp. 1694+99
HENDERSON, C. etc. 'The Proms', *Musical Opinion* 110 (November 1987), p. 350
MOORE, J.N. Sleeve note for ASD 2970 (1974)
MOORE, J.N. Sleeve note for CDM7 63133–2 (1989)
SANDERS, A. 'The Sanguine Fan', *Gramophone* 66 (May 1989), p. 1803

SCENES FROM THE BAVARIAN HIGHLANDS (Op. 27)

KELLER, H. 'Radio', *Musical Times* 123 (February 1982), p. 119

SCENES FROM THE SAGA OF KING OLAF (Op. 30)

ANON. ['As torrents in summer': review of publication], *Musical Times* 41 (February 1900), p. 103
ANON. [Footnote about the commission], *Musical Times* 36 (November 1895), p. 767
ANON. 'King Olaf ', *Music and Musicians* 25 (November 1976), p. 14+
ANON. 'King Olaf ', *Music and Musicians* 25 (February 1977), p. 46+
ANON. 'King Olaf ', *Musical Times* 118 (January 1977), p. 118
ANON. 'King Olaf in Australia: a brilliant success', *Musical Times* 39 (August 1898), p. 542
ANON. 'North Staffordshire Music Festival', *Musical Times* 37 (December 1896), pp. 805–806
ANON. [Reviews], *Musical Times* 39 (April 1898), p. 238
BENNETT, J. 'King Olaf ', *Daily Telegraph*, 31 October 1896, p. 5
BENNETT, J. 'Mr. Elgar's King Olaf ', *Musical Times* 37 (October 1896), pp. 668–69
BENNETT, J. 'Scenes from the Saga of King Olaf: Book of Words with Analytical Notes', London, Novello, 1899
GOODALL, J. 'Orchestral (London)', *Musical Times* 127 (January 1988), p. 39
KENNEDY, M. 'King Olaf ', *Gramophone* 64 (March 1987), pp. 1309–10
McVEAGH, D. 'Vocal: Elgar', *Musical Times* 115 (January 1974), pp. 59–60
MOORE, J.N. Sleeve note for CDS7 47659–8 (1987)
NEILL, A. The Saga of the recording of King Olaf ', *Elgar Society Journal* 5 (January 1987), pp. 8–10
NETTEL, R. [King Olaf: Elgar] *in* 'Music in the Five Towns, 1840–1914', London, Oxford University Press, 1944

NETTEL, R. [King Olaf: Elgar] *in* 'Ordeal by Music', London, Oxford University Press, 1945

POPE, M. 'King Olaf and the English Choral Tradition' *in* 'Elgar Studies' (ed. Raymond Monk), Aldershot, Scolar Press, 1990

RICHARDS, D. 'Elgar's King Olaf ', *Music and Musicians* 26 (July 1978), p. 49

SEA PICTURES (Op. 37)

ANON. 'Concerts', *Musical Opinion* 111 (May 1988), pp. 173–74

ANON. 'Norwich Music Festival', *Musical Times* 40 (November 1899), pp. 747–48

GREENFIELD, E. 'Sea Pictures', *Gramophone* 63 (May 1986), p. 1402

HARVEY, T. 'Sea Pictures', *Gramophone* 43 (December 1965), p. 294

SUTTON, W. 'Music and the sea', *Musical Opinion* 94 (June 1971), pp. 445–46

SERENADE FOR STRINGS (Op. 20)

BURNETT, G. Sleeve note for LXT 2699 (1952)

MACDONALD, M. 'Serenade for Strings', *Gramophone* 30 (September 1952), p. 81

SEVERN SUITE (Op. 87)

BRAND, G. 'The Severn Suite: whose scoring?' *British Bandsman*, 4 October 1980, pp. 12+17

CHISLETT, W.A. Sleeve note for ASD 2501 (1970)

GRACE, H. [Review of Suite, arranged for organ], *Musical Times* 73 (June 1932), p. 521

HARVEY, T. 'Severn Suite', *Gramophone* 47 (April 1970), p. 1589

JOHNSTON, M. 'Our status symbol', *Sound Brass* 1 (April 1972), pp. 9–10

KENNEDY, M. Sleeve note for CDM7 63280–2 (1990)

SANDERS, A. 'Elgar: orchestral works', *Gramophone* 67 (March 1990), p. 1603

SO MANY TRUE PRINCESSES

COLLETT, B. Sleeve note for SHE CD 9635 (1994)

KENT, C. 'Elgar's Queen Alexandra Memorial Ode', *Elgar Society Journal* 3 (January 1983), pp. 8–10

SOLILOQUY FOR OBOE

GREENFIELD, E. 'Soliloquy', *Gramophone* 54 (November 1976), p. 786

MARCH, I. 'Soliloquy', *Gramophone* 69 (February 1992), p. 98
MOORE, J.N. Sleeve note for LRL1 5133 (1976)
WYNNE, B. 'Soliloquy for oboe' *in* 'Music in the Wind', London, Souvenir Press, 1967

SONATA FOR ORGAN (Op. 28)

ANON. 'Elgar's Organ Sonata in G', *Organists Review* 75 no.4 (1989), pp. 251–55
BALDWYN, R. 'Elgar's Organ Sonata in G major', *Elgar Society Newsletter* no.8 (January 1976), pp. 23–27
BELLERBY, E.J. 'Elgar's Organ Sonata', *Music Student* 8 (August 1916), p. 373
KENT, C. 'Elgar's Organ Sonata in G (Op. 28): A study of the manuscript sources and original interpretation', *Journal of the British Institute of Organ Studies* 2 (1978), pp. 103 – 126
RIDGEWAY, J.C. 'Elgar's Organ Sonata', *Musical Times* 72 (April 1931), pp. 351–52
SMITH, R. 'Elgar's Organ Sonata', *Music (American Guild of Organists)* 7 (November 1973), pp. 32–33

SONATA FOR VIOLIN AND PIANO (Op. 82)

ANON. 'Elgar's new chamber music', *Musical Times* 60 (June 1919), p. 282
ANON. 'Elgar's Violin Sonata', *Musical Times* 60 (April 1919), pp. 162–63
COBBETT, W.W. [Sonata for Violin and Piano: Elgar] *in* 'Cobbett's Cyclopaedic Survey of Chamber Music', London, Oxford University Press, 1929
HARVEY, B. 'The Elgar Sonata on record', *Strad* 93 (March 1983), pp. 792–93
KEYS, I. 'Ghostly Stuff: The Brinkwells Music' *in* 'Edward Elgar: Music and Literature' (ed. Raymond Monk), Aldershot, Scolar Press, 1993
REED, W.H., etc. 'London Concerts: Elgar's Violin Sonata', *Musical Times* 60 (April 1919), p. 179

SOSPIRI (Op. 70)

HARVEY, T. 'Sospiri', *Gramophone* 44 (December 1966), pp. 315–16

THE SPANISH LADY

HARVEY, T. 'The Spanish Lady', *Gramophone* 46 (October 1968), p. 503
JACKSON, B. 'The Spanish Lady', *Music and Letters* 24 (January 1943), pp. 1–14
JACKSON, S. Sleeve note for LOND 421–384–2LM (1989)
JOHNSON, S. 'Orchestral (London)', *Musical Times* 127 (July 1986), p. 398
McVEAGH, D. Sleeve note for RG573 (1968)
ROSE, B.W.G. [Review of the score], *Music and Letters* 37 (October 1956), p. 412

ROWLEY, A. [Review of two songs, edited by Percy Young], *Musical Times* 97 (February 1956), p. 84

SANDERS, A. 'The Spanish Lady', *Gramophone* 67 (August 1989), p. 370

YOUNG, P.M. 'Elgar and the Spanish Lady', *Musical Times* 127 (May 1986), pp. 272–76

THE SPIRIT OF ENGLAND (Op. 80)

ANON. 'A memorable musical event', *Musical Times* 57 (June 1916), p. 296

ANON. 'Occasional Notes', *Musical Times* 60 (January 1919), p. 21

HARVEY, T. 'The Spirit of England', *Gramophone* 54 (May 1977), pp. 1718+23

McELHERAN, B. 'Edward Elgar's The Spirit of England', *Choral Journal* 22 no.5 (1982), pp. 38–39

MARCH, I. 'The Spirit of England', *Gramophone* 70 (November 1992), p. 240

MOORE, J.N. Sleeve note for CHAN 6574 (1992)

MOORE, J.N. Sleeve note for RL 25074 (1977)

KOVALENKO, S.C. 'The twentieth century requiem: an emerging concept', Ph.D. thesis, University of Washington, 1971

NEWMAN, E. 'Elgar's Fourth of August', *Musical Times* 58 (July 1917), pp. 295–97

NEWMAN, E. 'The Spirit of England', *Musical Times* 57 (May 1916), pp. 235–39

NORRIS, G. 'Elgar', *Musical Times* 121 (September 1980), p. 574

SANDERS, A. 'The Spirit of England', *Gramophone* 65 (August 1987), p. 338

THE STARLIGHT EXPRESS (Op. 78)

ANON. 'The Starlight Express: music by Sir Edward Elgar', *Musical Times* 57 (February 1916), p. 95

ASHMORE, B. 'Correspondence: Elgar's The Starlight Express', *Gramophone* 54 (June 1976), p. 91

KEETON, A.E. 'Music for The Starlight Express', *Music and Letters* 26 (January 1945), pp. 43–46

McVEAGH, D. 'Starlight Express', *Musical Times* 120 (March 1979), p. 239

MARCH, I. 'The Starlight Express', *Gramophone* 67 (January 1990), p. 1361

MARCH, I. 'The Starlight Express' Gramophone 71 (November 1993), p. 168

MOORE, J.N. Sleeve note for CHAN 6582 (1993)

MOORE, J.N. Sleeve note for SQ SLS 5036 (1976)

MOORE, J.N. 'The Starlight Express', Sleeve notes for SLS 5036 (1976)

SALTER, L. 'The Starlight Express', *Gramophone* 53 (May 1976), p. 1757

SIMMONS, K.E.L. 'Elgar and the Wonderful Stranger: Music for the Starlight Express' *in* 'Elgar Studies' (ed. Raymond Monk), Aldershot, Scolar Press, 1990

WIMBUSH, R. 'Here and there', *Gramophone* 51 (August 1973), pp. 326–28

SYMPHONY NO 1 (Op. 55)

ANON. 'Editorial Notes', *Strad* 88 (November 1977), p. 581

ANON. 'Elgar music in Rome', *Musical Times* 51 (February 1910), p. 108

ANON. 'Elgar's Symphony', *Musical Times* 50 (February 1909), p. 102

ANON. 'Elgar's Symphony – first performances in Manchester and London', *Musical Times* 50 (January 1909), pp. 24–25

ANON. 'Sir Edward Elgar's Symphony', *Musical Times* 49 (December 1908), pp. 778–80

ANON. 'Proms '89', *Musical Opinion* 112 (December 1989), p. 426

ANON. 'Recordings in review', *Musical America* 107 no.5 (1987), p. 60

ANON. [Symphony No.1 in Ab major], *Boston Symphony Orchestra Program Notes* 26 February 1970, pp. 12 – 13

BONAVIA, F. [Edward Elgar] in 'The Symphony' (ed. R. Hill), London, Penguin, 1949

BRIAN, H. 'Letters to the editor: Mr. T. Beecham and Elgar's Symphony', *Musical Times* 50 (December 1909), p. 793

BUCKHALTER, E. 'Edward Elgar: Symphony No.1 in Ab major (Op. 55): A Comparative Review', *Elgar Society Newsletter* no.4 (September 1974), pp. 18–24

COLLES, H.C. 'Sir Edward Elgar's Symphony', *Musical Times* 49 (December 1908), pp. 778–800

COX, D. [Edward Elgar] in 'The Symphony' (ed. R.Simpson), Volume 2 Harmondsworth, Penguin, 1967

FISKE, R. 'Elgar's Symphonies', *Gramophone* 46 (October 1968), pp. 500+503

GODDARD, S. Sleeve note for ALP 1989/ASD 540 (1963)

HALL, D. 'Elgar's Symphony No.1', *Stereo Review* 40 (June 1978), p. 146

HARVEY, T. 'Symphony No.1', *Gramophone* 35 (September 1957), p. 136

HARVEY, T. 'Symphony No.1', *Gramophone* 41 (October 1963), p. 182

HILL, E.W. 'Elgar's Symphony No.1: a point of interpretation', *Musical Times* 81 (July 1940), p. 317

JACOBSON, B. 'Edward Elgar', *Stereo Review* 30 (May 1973), p. 112

KENNEDY, M. Sleeve note for CCL 30102/3 (1957)

KENNEDY, M. Sleeve note for CDM7 64511–2 (1993)

KENNEDY, M. Sleeve note for SRCS 39/40 (1968)

MEIKLE, R. 'The True Foundation: the Symphonies' in 'Edward Elgar: Music and Literature' (ed. Raymond Monk), Aldershot, Scolar Press, 1993

NEWMAN, E. 'Elgar's Symphonies at Birmingham', *Musical Times* 53 (July 1912), p. 456 (Reprinted from *The Birmingham Post*)

PIRIE, P. J. 'Gramophone recordings: Elgar conducts Elgar', *Music Review* 33 no.1 (1972), pp. 76–80

SECKERSON, E. 'Symphony No.1', *Gramophone* 71 (June 1993), p. 40

WELLS-HARRISON, W. 'The Elgar Symphonies', *Music Student* 8 (August 1916), p. 351–353

WESTBROOK, F.B. 'Reflections on Elgar's First Symphony', *Elgar Society Newsletter* no.10 (September 1976), pp. 26–29

WORDSWORTH, W.B. 'Scoring of Elgar's First Symphony', *Musical Times* 80 (May 1939), p. 379

SYMPHONY NO. 2 (Op. 63)

ACHENBACH, A. 'Elgar's Second Symphony', *Gramophone* 71 (September 1993), pp. 28–29

ANON. 'An American critic on the Elgar Symphony', *Musical Times* 51 (January 1910), pp. 19–20

ANON. 'Classical reviews', *HiFi* 39 (June 1989), pp. 64–65

ANON. 'Elgar's Edwardian Symphony No.2', *American Record Guide* 21 (August 1955), p. 380

ANON. 'The London Music Festival', *Musical Times* 52 (June 1911), p. 381

ANON. 'Occasional notes: premiere of Nikisch's performances in Germany', *Musical Times* 52 (July 1911), p. 454

ANON. 'Opus record reviews' *Musical America* 109 no.4 (1989), pp. 55–56

ANON. 'Recordings in review', *Musical America* 107 no.5 (1987), p. 60

ANON. [Symphony No.2], *New York Philharmonic Program Notes* 6 January 1966, pp. B-C

BONAVIA, F. [Edward Elgar] *in* 'The Symphony' (ed. R.Hill), London, Penguin, 1949

COX, D. 'Edward Elgar' *in* 'The Symphony' (ed. R.Simpson) Volume 2, Harmondsworth, Penguin, 1967

GAIRDNER, W.H. Temple (Canon) 'Elgar's Second Symphony' *in* 'W.H.T.G. to his friends', London, S.P.C.K., 1930

GIMBEL, A. 'Elgar's Prize Song: Quotation and Allusion in the Second Symphony', *Nineteenth Century Music* 12 no.3 (Spring 1989), pp. 231–240

GREW, S. 'Elgar's Second Symphony', *Musical Opinion* 37 (January 1914), p. 247; (February 1914), p. 320

HALL, D. 'Elgar's Second by Boult: a realization as close to perfect as it is ever likely to be', *Stereo Review* 38 (May 1977), p. 77

HARVEY, T. 'Symphony No.2', *Gramophone* 42 (December 1964), p. 282

JACOBSON, B. 'Edward Elgar', *Stereo Review* 30 (May 1973), p. 112

KENNEDY, M. Sleeve note for CDM7 64724–2 (1994)

KENT, C. 'A view of Elgar's methods of composition through the sketches of Symphony No.2 in Eb major (Op. 63)', *Proceedings of the Royal Musical Association* 103 (1976/77), pp. 41–60

McKAY, M. Sleeve note for ALP 2061/2 ASD610–11 (1964)

McNAUGHT, W. 'A note on Elgar's Second Symphony', *Musical Times* 92 (February 1951), pp. 57–61

MEIKLE, R. 'The True Foundation: the Symphonies' *in* 'Edward Elgar: Music and Literature' (ed. Raymond Monk), Aldershot, Scolar Press, 1993

MORLEY, C. 'Letters to the editor: Elgar's Liebestod?', *Musical Times* 123 (April 1982), p. 241

NEWMAN, E. 'Elgar's Second Symphony', *Musical Times* 52 (May 1911), pp. 295–300

NEWMAN, E. 'Elgar's Symphonies at Birmingham', *Musical Times* 53 (July 1912), p. 456 (Reprinted from *The Birmingham Post*)

PAYNE, A. 'Elgar's Second,' *Music and Musicians* 11 (May 1963), p. 42

PIRIE, P.J. 'Gramophone recordings: Elgar conducts Elgar', *Music Review* 33 no.1 (1972), pp. 76–80

SECKERSEN, E. 'Symphony No.2', *Gramophone* 71 (February 1994), p. 40

SHORE, B. [Elgar's Second Symphony] *in* 'Sixteen Symphonies', London, Longman, 1949

SIMMONS, D. 'Concert notes', *Strad* 78 (February 1968), p. 395

TOVEY, D.F. [Elgar: Symphony No. 2] *in* 'Essays in Musical Analysis' Volume 2: Symphonies London, Oxford University Press, 1935–39

WELLS-HARRISON, W. 'The Elgar Symphonies', *Music Student* 8 (August 1916), pp. 351–353

WESTBROOK, F.B. 'Edwardianism and Elgar's Second Symphony', *Musical Times* 92 (May 1951), pp. 224–25

SYMPHONY NO.3 (Op. 88)

ANON. 'Elgar's unfinished'. *Musical Times* 76 (October 1935), p. 883

BURTON, H. 'Elgar and the BBC', *Musical Opinion* 103 (December 1979), pp. 84–89 + 91

BURTON, H. 'Elgar and the BBC with particular reference to the unfinished Third Symphony', *Journal of the Royal Society of Arts* 127 (March 1979), pp. 224 – 236

FISKE, R. 'Correspondence: Elgar's Third Symphony' *Gramophone* 53 (July 1975), p. 274

GOLDSTONE, H. 'Correspondence: Elgar's Third Symphony', *Gramophone* 53 (June 1975), p. 133

KENT, C. 'Elgar's Third Symphony: the sketches reconsidered', *Musical Times* 123 (August 1982), pp. 532–537

MAINE, B. 'Elgar's sketches in relation to musicology' *in* 'Basil Maine on Music', London, Westhouse, 1945

NEWMAN, E. 'Elgar's Third Symphony', *The Sunday Times*, 22 September 1935, p. 5; 27 October 1935, p. 5

POSSELWHITE, E.R. 'Correspondence: Boult and Elgar', *Gramophone* 52 (April 1975), p. 1901

REED, W.H. 'Elgar's Third Symphony', *The Listener*, 28 August 1935. This article was also published separately in London (1935) and according to the British Museum catalogue is 'Supplement no.24' to *The Listener*.

REED, W.H. [Symphony No.3] *in* 'Elgar as I knew him', London, Gollancz, 1936

WALKER, R. 'The final enigma', *Music and Musicians* 23 (May 1975), p. 16+

TE DEUM AND BENEDICTUS (Op. 34)

ANON. 'Festival of the Three Choirs', *Musical Times* 38 (October 1897), pp. 667–78
KENNEDY, M. 'Te Deum and Benedictus', *Gramophone* 64 (March 1987), pp. 1309–10
SANDERS, A. 'Te Deum and Benedictus', *Gramophone* 65 (August 1987), p. 338
MOORE, J.N. Sleeve note for CDC7 47658–2 (1987)

THREE CHARACTERISTIC PIECES (Op. 10)

ANON. 'Music in Birmingham', *Musical Times* 29 (April 1888), pp. 229–230
ANON. [Review of the score], *Musical Times* 40 (August 1899), p. 551
POTTER, T. 'Record Reviews', *Strad* 100 (July 1989), p. 589

TO HER, BENEATH WHOSE STEADFAST STAR

ANON. 'An Elgar concert at Windsor', *Musical Times* 40 (November 1899), p. 758
ANON. 'The Queen's 80th birthday celebrations' Musical Times 40 (June 1899), pp. 388–89

TWO SONGS (Op. 60)

ANON. 'Two songs for medium voice', *Musical Opinion* 79 (October 1955), p. 29

UN VOIX DANS LE DÉSERT (Op. 77)

ANON. 'New work by Sir Edward Elgar', *Musical Times* 57 (March 1916), pp. 155–56
COLLETT, B. Sleeve note for SHE CD 9602 (1988)
KENNEDY, M. Sleeve note for ASD 3050 (1975)
MOORE, J.N. 'Un voix dans le désert', *Gramophone* 52 (February 1975), p. 1491
SANDERS, A. 'Un voix dans le désert', *Gramophone* 65 (May 1988), p. 1628

VARIATIONS ON AN ORIGINAL THEME (ENIGMA) (Op. 36)

ANON. 'Classical recordings,' *Fanfare* 4 no.1 (1980), pp. 114–117
ANON. 'Elgar's new variations', *Musical Times* 40 (July 1899), pp. 464+471

ANON. 'Music in Bristol', *Musical Times* 40 (January 1899), pp. 39–40

ANON. 'Notes', *Musical Times* 40 (March 1899), p. 161

ANON. 'Notes and News', *Musical Times* 79 (December 1938), p. 932

ANON. 'Notes and News: An unknown Enigma', *Musical Times* 75 (August 1934), p. 735

ANON. 'Notes and News: the Enigma solution?' *Musical Times* 80 (June 1939), p. 456

ANON. 'Occasional Notes', *Musical Times* 41 (November 1900), p. 165

ANON. 'Occasional Notes', *Musical Times* 43 (January 1902), p. 23

ANON. 'The Proms', *Musical Opinion* 112 (January 1989), p. 24

ANON. 'Records: Enigma Variations', *Ballet News* 2 (January 1981), p. 33

ANON. [Review of Intermezzo arranged for piano], *Musical Times* 42 (March 1901), p. 185

ANON. [Review of publications], *Musical Times* 40 (September 1899), p. 620

ANON. [Variations for Orchestra], *Boston Symphony Orchestra Concert Bulletin* no.13 (22 January 1954), pp. 612–18

ANON. [Variations for Orchestra], *Cincinnati Symphony Orchestra Program Notes*, 1 December 1950, pp. 214–21

ANON. [Variations for Orchestra], *Cincinnati Symphony Orchestra Program Notes*, 16 October 1953, pp. 50–55

ANON. [Variations for Orchestra], *Cincinnati Symphony Orchestra Program Notes*, 7 October 1955, pp. 18–24

ANON. [Variations for Orchestra], *Cincinnati Symphony Orchestra Program Notes*, 14 February 1958, pp. 581–84+

ANON. [Variations for Orchestra], *Houston Symphony Orchestra Program Notes*, 15 October 1962, p. 15+

ANON. [Variations for Orchestra], *Los Angeles Philharmonic Orchestra Symphony Magazine*, 16–17 February 1950, p. 465+

ANON. [Variations for Orchestra], *Los Angeles Philharmonic Orchestra Symphony Magazine*, 17 January 1952, p. 17+

ANON. [Variations for Orchestra], *Philadelphia Orchestra Program Notes* 1 January 1954, pp. 325–29+

ANON. [Variations for Orchestra], *San Francisco Symphony Orchestra Program Notes*, 4 December 1957, p. 31+

ANON. [Variations for Orchestra], *San Francisco Symphony Orchestra Program Notes*, 25 January 1962, pp. 25–32

ANON. [Variations: letters to the editor], *Musical Times* 111 (January 1970), pp. 39–40

ATKINS, I. 'Elgar's Enigma Variations', *Musical Times* 75 (April 1934), pp. 328–30 (May 1934), pp. 411–14

BARBER, C. 'Enigma Variations: an earlier ending', *Music and Letters* 16 (April 1935), pp. 137–38

BOFFINS, D.I. 'Letters to the editor: Enigma solution?' *Musical Times* 80 (January 1939), p. 59

BOFFINS, D.I. 'Letters to the editor: Enigma solution?' *Musical Times* 80 (March 1939), p. 215

BOOKSPAN, M. 'The basic repertoire', *HiFi/Stereo Review* 16 (January 1966), pp. 39–40

BOZMAN, E.F. 'Correspondence: the Enigma Variations', *Music and Letters* 44 (January 1963), p. 98

BREWER, A.H. [Enigma Variations] *in* 'Memories of Choirs and Cloisters . . .' London, Lane, 1931

ELGAR, E.W. 'Audiographic Music Rolls: Elgar explains the Enigma Variations', *British Musician*, January 1930, p. 16

ELGAR, E.W. 'My friends pictured within', London, Novello, 1929

ELGAR, E.W. 'My friends pictured within', *About the House* 2 no.12 (1968), pp. 46–49

ELGAR, E.W. Programme note for the first performance of the Enigma Variations (Op. 36), 19 June 1899

ELKIN, R. 'The Enigma Variations', *Music in Education* 26 (15 July 1962), pp. 95–96

FISKE, R. 'The Enigma: a solution', *Musical Times* 110 (November 1969), pp. 1124–26

FISKE, R. 'Enigma Variations', *Gramophone* 35 (July 1957), p. 54

FOX-STRANGWAYS, A.H. 'The Enigma' (correspondence), *Music and Letters* 16 (January 1935), pp. 37–39

GOODWIN, N. 'Elgarian enigma', *Music and Musicians* 11 (April 1963), pp. 14–15

HOGAN, E.E. 'A musical detective story – after 75 years: the solution of Elgar's Enigma', *Musical Opinion* 99 (November 1975), pp. 75–77

HOUTEN, T. VAN 'You of all people: Elgar's Enigma', *Music Review* 37 (May 1976), pp. 130–142

HOWES, F. 'The unknown Enigma', *Musical Times* 75 (October 1934), pp. 933–34

HUDSON, D. 'Elgar's Enigma: the trail of evidence', *Musical Times* 125 (November 1984), pp. 636–639

JONES, T.F. 'The Duo Art Pianola Rolls of the Enigma Variations', *Elgar Society Newsletter* no.6 (May 1975), pp. 17–22

KENNEDY, M. Sleeve note for CCL 30101 (1957)

KINGDON, B. 'The Enigma: a hidden dark saying', *Elgar Society Journal* 1 (May 1979), pp. 9–12

KOEGLER, H. 'Ashton's neues Ballett', *Musica* 23 no.2 (1969), p. 131

KOLODIN, I. 'Two musical riddles resolved (partially)', *World* 2 (17 July 1973), p. 54

KOLODIN, I. 'What is the enigma?' *Saturday Review* 36 (28 February 1953), p. 53+

KOLODIN, I. 'Winners of the Enigma contest', *Saturday Review* 36 (30 May 1953), p. 48+

LORENZ, R. 'Enigma Variations: a different approach' Part 1 – Literary, *Musical Opinion* 58 (December 1934), pp. 212–213; Part 2 – *Musical Opinion* 58 (January 1935), pp. 311–312

McVEAGH, D. 'Ashton's Enigma Ballet', *Musical Times* 109 (December 1968), p. 1129

McVEAGH, D. 'Music in London', *Musical Times* 109 (December 1968), pp. 1129–1130

MOORE, J.N. 'An approach to Elgar's Enigma', *Music Review* 20 (February 1959), pp. 28–44

NEWMAN, E. 'A dissertation on dots – Elgar's second enigma' *Sunday Times*, 21 May 1939

NEWMAN, E. 'Elgar and his Enigma', *Sunday Times*, 16 April 1939, p. 5; 23 April 1939, p. 5; 30 April 1939, p. 5; 7 May 1939, p. 7

PARROTT, I. 'Elgar's two-fold enigma: a religious sequel' *Music and Letters* 54 (January 1973), pp. 57–60

PARROTT, I. 'The Enigma' *in* 'An Elgar Companion' (ed. C.Redwood), Ashbourne, Sequoia, 1982

PARROTT, I. 'Letters to the editor: Enigma solution?' *Musical Times* 80 (February 1939), p. 135

PIDCOCK, G.D.H. 'Letters to the editor: An Enigma detail', *Musical Times* 75 (May 1934), p. 451

POOLE, G. 'Questioning the Enigma', *Music and Musicians* 19 (August 1971), pp. 26–29

PORTER, A. 'Enigma Variations' (ballet), *Financial Times*, 28 October 1968 Reprinted in *About the House* 3 no.1 (1969), pp. 14–19

PORTNOY, M.A. 'The answer to Elgar's Enigma', *Musical Quarterly* 71 no.2 (1985), pp. 205–210

POWELL, R.C. 'Elgar's Enigma', *Music and Letters* 15 (July 1934), pp. 203–8

POWELL, R.C. 'Letters to the editor: Enigma solution?' *Musical Times* 80 (January 1939), p. 61

POWELL, R.C. 'Letters to the editor: the unknown Elgar', *Musical Times* 75 (September 1934), pp. 835–36

REED, N. 'Elgar's enigmatic inamorata', *Musical Times* 125 (August 1984), pp. 430–34

SAMS, E. 'Variations on an original theme', *Musical Times* 111 (March 1970), pp. 258–262

SKOUENBORG, U. 'Elgar's Enigma: the solution', *Music Review* 43 (August–November 1982), pp. 160–168

SWINYARD, L. 'Analytical notes on Elgar's Enigma Variations', London, Novello, 1961

TREND, M. 'The enigma unexplained', *Times Literary Supplement*, 15 July 1983, p. 751

WAINE, F. 'Letters to the editor: Enigma solution?' *Musical Times* 80 (January 1939), pp. 59–60

WESTRUP, J.A. 'Elgar's Enigma', *Royal Musical Association Proceedings* no.86 (23 April 1960), pp. 79–97

WHITE, R.T. 'Elgar's Enigma Variations', *Music Student*, 16 (May 1924), p. 296

WHITTEN, D.J. 'Letters: pop goes the Enigma', *Music and Musicians* 26 (December 1977), pp. 4–5

YOUNG, P.M. 'Friends Pictured Within' *in* 'Elgar Studies' (ed. Raymond Monk), Aldershot, Scolar Press, 1990

THE WAND OF YOUTH SUITE No.1 (Op. 1a)

ANDERSON, W.R. 'Wand of Youth Suite No.1', *Gramophone* 28 (December 1950), p. 141

ANON. 'Occasional notes', *Musical Times* 47 (December 1907), p. 784

ELGAR, E.W. 'The Wand of Youth: a note by the composer [for H.M.V. Album 80]', London, The Gramophone Company, 1929

THE WAND OF YOUTH SUITE No.2 (Op. 1b)

ANON. 'Queen's Hall Orchestra', *Musical Times* 49 (November 1908), p. 728

ANON. [The Wand of Youth Suite No.2], *New York Philharmonic Program Notes*, 21 June 1966

ANON. 'Worcester Music Festival', *Musical Times* 49 (October 1908), p. 646

BONAVIA, F. 'Elgar's Wand of Youth in play form at Malvern', *Musical Times* 71 (November 1930), p. 1035

ELGAR, E.W. Programme note for the first performance of the Wand of Youth Suite No.2, 9 September 1908

KEYS, I. [Review of Suites 1 and 2], *Music and Letters* 31 (October 1950), p. 374

WITH PROUD THANKSGIVING

LLOYD, S. 'Eton', *Musical Times* 129 (December 1988), p. 680

ZUT! ZUT! ZUT!

ANON. 'Reviews', *Musical Times* 65 (July 1924), p. 619

General Index

This index contains personal and other names which appear in the chronology and the sections on works and performances, recordings and collections. Only works and personal names appearing in the titles of articles cited in the bibliography are also included.